The Earliest Fife Football Clubs

James K. Corstorphine

Nineteenth Century Football in the Kingdom of Fife

Published by:

Wast-By Books
26 Friday Walk
Lower Largo
Fife
Scotland
KY8 6FB

Text Copyright © 2018 James K. Corstorphine

All rights reserved

ISBN: 9781980249580

No part of this publication may be reproduced, stored in a retrieval system or transmitted in any form or by any means without the prior permission of the publisher.

This book is based on a series of articles, written by the author, titled *"Early Fife Football Clubs"*, which appeared in the official match-day magazine of East Fife Football Club, *'The Bayview'*, during the 2016/17 football season.

Front Cover: Cellardyke Bluejackets with the Martin White Cup

By the same author:

On That Windswept Plain: The First One Hundred Years of East Fife Football Club
(ISBN 9781976888618)

Our Boys and the Wise Men: The Origins of Dundee Football Club
(ISBN 9798643521549)

East of Thornton Junction: The Story of the FifeCoast Line
(ISBN 9781976909283)

Peter Smith, the Fisherman Poet of Cellardyke
(ISBN 9798644727827)

All of the above titles are available in both paperback and Kindle eBook format from amazon.co.uk

The Cellardyke Bluejackets

Written in the 'auld Scots tongue' by the celebrated Fife bard 'Poetry Peter' Smith, the following lines recalling the very early days of football in the Fife fishing village of Cellardyke were extracted from his poem "Tae Jeems".

As long's my memory has the knack,
Tae mind o' yon days far, far back.
Whar the "Bluejackets" had their pitch,
Are hooses noo, for puir or rich,
I, and you tae, can mind it fine,
Tam Dug ran doon along the line,
And no a man hooever swift,
But Tam could left far oot o' sicht.
Nae doot, time wi' its magic wand,
Has made thae auld days look mair graund,
Yet tho' we see them - throo' a mist,
Thae days tae us - are ever bless't,
And when the Crailers cam' tae play,
The hale Toll Road was fu' that day,
Hoo little Duggie taen the lead,
Coupit lang Morris ower his heid,
Hoo you and Crieff fair had the knack,
Tae mak' wha e'er cam' near - stout back,
Whiteheid, in Dyker fitba' story,
As famous as the great McGrory,
A heid as hard as stane, or coal,
Gar'd the ba' stout frae goal tae goal,
Big Mitchell in the goal - sic knocks,
His neeves like twa fore haulyard blocks.

Contents

	Page
Introduction	7
Dunfermline F.C.	9
Burntisland Thistle	13
Cameron Bridge F.C.	21
Kirkcaldy Wanderers	25
Wemyss F.C.	33
Lassodie F.C.	37
The First Tayport Clubs	45
Star of Leven and Vale of Leven	49
Strathforth F.C.	53
Vale of Eden	57
The First Kirkcaldy Junior Clubs	61
Cellardyke Bluejackets	67
Crail Union	73
Binnend Rangers	77
AncientCity Athletic	81
Leven F.C.	91
Lochgelly United	95
Other Notable Nineteenth Century Fife Football Clubs	105
Former Fife Association Members from Neighbouring Counties	112

Introduction

The history of football clubs founded in the nineteenth century is a fascinating subject. As the popularity of Association Football spread from the west of Scotland through to the east during the 1870's, several clubs were founded in Fife, initially in the west and central Fife coal-mining communities, before spreading to the far-eastern parts of the County during the 1880's.

The development of the railway network throughout Fife during the mid-to-late nineteenth century; the improvement of the road system, and the gradual introduction of more leisure time, made it far easier for the working classes to commute between the towns and villages, which in turn meant that competitive sports meetings between rival communities were now more feasible.

As this book reveals, these rivalries could be rather fierce where football clubs were concerned!

This book details the history of several of these early football clubs, but it by no means covers the history of every team founded in Fife during the late 1800's.

The football clubs whose histories are detailed on the following pages are the clubs which, in the opinion of the writer, are the ones with the most interesting tales to tell!

The club histories have been set out in chronological order; from Dunfermline F.C., founded in 1874, through to Lochgelly United, founded in 1890.

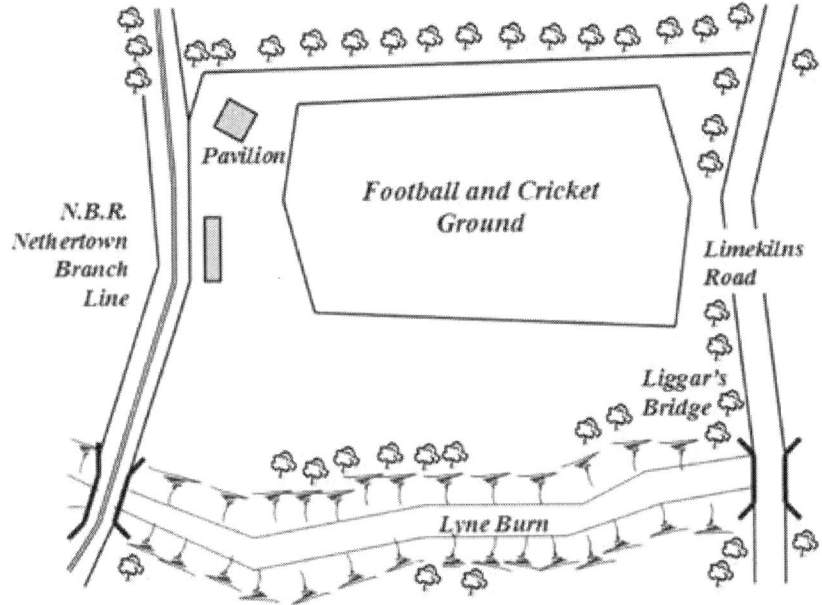

LadysmillPark, the home of Dunfermline Football Club from 1879 until the club eventually folded in 1901. The ground boasted a grandstand as well as a pavilion in the north-west corner. Today, the ground is known as McKanePark, and is the home of both DunfermlineRugby Club and Dunfermline & Carnegie Cricket Club.

Dunfermline F.C.

Dunfermline Football Club was founded in 1874 and, although they never tasted any real success as a senior outfit, they will go down in history as being the first Fife club to compete in the Scottish Cup.

The writer would also like to point out at this stage that Dunfermline F.C., whose colours were blue and white hoops with navy shorts, are not the black and white striped Dunfermline Athletic we are familiar with today, although the two clubs did have a very strong connection in the early years of the game!

Dunfermline Football Club was originally formed as a subsidiary of Dunfermline Cricket Club, in order to keep the cricketers fit during the winter months. Before long, however, footballers who had no connection with the cricket club began to force their way into the football team, much to the exasperation of the original club members. The result was that a new rule was implemented stating that only members of the cricket club could play for the football team. The footballers who were, as a result, ousted from the team, decided to set up a club of their own, which resulted in the foundation of Dunfermline Athletic in 1885.

Originally, Dunfermline Football Club played on the Town's Green (near the present-day East EndPark), an arrangement which continued until 1879, when they re-located to Ladysmill on the south-west side of the town. The football and cricket ground at Ladysmill was sandwiched between the now-defunct Nethertown Branch of the North British Railway and the Limekilns Road, just to the north of Liggar's Bridge. Today the ground is known as McKanePark and is the home of both Dunfermline Rugby Club and Dunfermline & Carnegie Cricket Club.

After Dunfermline F.C. moved into Ladysmill in 1879, the ground was gradually improved, and by the 1890's the pitch had been enclosed and boasted a grandstand and a pavilion in the north-west corner.

The club first entered the Scottish Cup in 1876, when they were drawn to face Hearts at home in the first round of the competition, and progressed to round two by way of a "walk-over". The reason for the tie being decided in this manner is not clear, as it was not mentioned in any of the newspapers of the day; football being regarded as a minority sport in the 1870's. Indeed, perusal of the 'Scotsman' on the Monday following the scheduled match, which had been due to be played on 30th September 1876, reveals that the sports columns were entirely devoted to horse racing, golf, bowling, angling and partridge shooting!

In round two, Dunfermline were drawn away to Hamilton Accies, where the club's interest in their inaugural venture into the Scottish Cup was ended with a 2-1 defeat.

The following season, Dunfermline were drawn to face Dundee side St Clement's in Dundee on 29th September 1877, but subsequently withdrew from the competition for reasons unknown.

A year later, the first round of the national competition saw the Fife club drawn to face Hibernian at Powderhall, where the Edinburgh side won by five goals to two; the score-line having been kept respectable, according to the 'Scotsman', by "the watchfulness of the Dunfermline goal keeper".

Season 1879/80 saw Dunfermline record their first actual victory in the Scottish Cup when Edinburgh Thistle were beaten 2-1 at Ladysmill, but interest in the competition was ended again by Hibs in the second round, this time by four goals without reply.

Subsequent seasons proved to be no better, with the club never managing to progress beyond the second round of the competition. After the newly-founded Dunfermline Athletic entered the Scottish Cup in 1885, Dunfermline F.C.'s interest in the competition started to wane, and for two successive years, in 1888 and 1889, when the two local rivals were drawn to face each other, Dunfermline F.C. scratched to the now-stronger Athletic before the ties were even played!

Thus ended Dunfermline Football Club's interest in the Scottish Cup, as they did not enter the competition in subsequent seasons.

As Dunfermline Athletic continued to grow from strength to strength, the opposite could be said of Dunfermline F.C., and in 1891 the club decided to relinquish its senior status and become a junior club.

The only competitions they entered during their first two seasons in the junior ranks were in the Scottish Junior Cup, the Dunfermline Cup, the Kirkcaldy Cup and the Cowdenbeath Cup, but in 1893 Dunfermline decided to join Fife Junior League, where they competed alongside Methil Rovers, Pathhead United, Blairadam, Hearts of Beath, Lassodie and Lochgelly Rangers, as well as the junior sides affiliated to Cowdenbeath and Dunfermline Athletic.

The following season, the club asserted its standing in Fife junior circles by winning the Fife Junior League at only the second time of asking. Dunfermline remained members of the Fife Junior League until the end of the 1899/1900 season; during which time they competed alongside the teams previously mentioned as well as Ancient City Athletic (from St Andrews), Buckhaven United, Cupar Athletic, Kirkcaldy Albion, Raith Athletic, Donibristle Heatherbell, Inverkeithing Thistle and Markinch Albion.

The 1896/97 season saw Dunfermline embark on their best-ever run in the Scottish Junior Cup, when they reached the final (the first Fife club to do so!) following seven grueling rounds, only to lose to Glasgow side Strathclyde by the odd-goal-in-five at Parkhead on Saturday 8th May 1897. Dunfermline protested the outcome, and initially it was decided by the SJFA that the final be replayed, but unfortunately a subsequent appeal by Strathclyde was upheld, and the cup remained in Glasgow. Dunfermline reached the fifth round of the Scottish Cup on two subsequent occasions; in 1899/1900, when the club lost out again to Strathclyde in front of Ladysmill's record attendance for a junior match of 1,500 on 4th March 1900; and again the following season.

During season 1899/1900, Dunfermline played simultaneously in the Fife Junior League and the East of Scotland Junior League, but the following season the club left the Fife Junior League to concentrate on the East of Scotland competition alongside Our Boys and Vale of Grange from Bo'ness, Edinburgh Renton, Musselburgh Fern, Niddrie Violet and University Athletic.

Rather surprisingly, just as it looked like Dunfermline Juniors were about to establish themselves in the higher echelons of Scottish Junior Football, the club folded in April 1901.
The demise of the first Fife club to compete in the Scottish Cup and the first Fife club to reach the final of the Scottish Junior Cup is surrounded in mystery, but could well be connected in some way with the foundation of junior sides Dunfermline Our Boys and Dunfermline Violet, who were inaugurated around the same time.

Burntisland Thistle

Burntisland Thistle were one of Fife's earliest football clubs, having been founded in the late 1870's. Some sources record the year of the club's foundation to be as early as 1877, but the first mention of any match played by Burntisland Thistle in the local press was during season 1879/80, when they played at least two matches against the east of Fife's first football club, Cameron Bridge FC.

There was, however, an earlier match played during the previous season on Burntisland Green between two local teams; one called Burntisland and the other called Thistle; which inspired one appreciative spectator to submit a poem to the following edition of the 'Fifeshire Advertiser' to commemorate the first goal. This lengthy poem, written in that style so typical of a bygone age, concluded:

> *"With all their men their man they follow quick,*
> *Till through the posts the rolling ball they kick.*
> *Thus their first goal the valiant Thistle won –*
> *Two more they gained before the game was done."*

Thistle became firmly established on the Fife football map over the following few seasons, and in 1882 were one of the founding members of the Fifeshire Football Association along with local rivals Rossend FC.

The Fifeshire Football Association was responsible for the inauguration of the Fife Cup, but Thistle rarely progressed beyond the early rounds of the competition during its formative years. In season 1886/87, however, the club embarked on a Fife Cup run that saw the team literally "do battle" with Lumphinnans and Cowdenbeath en-route to the final, where it took three hostile clashes with Dunfermline Athletic before the destiny of the trophy was decided.

Initially, Burntisland Thistle played their home matches on Burntisland Links, but the ground had the disadvantage of having to be shared with the local golfers, as is evident from the following comment which appeared in the local press following a home game against CameronBridge:

"It is to be regretted that the game of golf is conducted on the same ground, and the golf ball sometimes interferes with the play of those who follow the football at Burntisland. Separate ranges for each would be a great advantage to the patrons of both sports."

In 1885, Burntisland Thistle merged with local rivals Rossend, but retained the Thistle name. The reason for this merger would appear to be down to the fact that Thistle had recently tempted four Rossend players to join them, including the formidable MacKenzie triplets, who commanded the goal and full-back positions.

This consequently weakened the Rossend side to the point that it would have been futile to carry on, and a merger with their rivals was the only viable alternative. The club also relocated to Lammerlaws point, a promontory on the east side of the docks, at this time. Before the end of the year, the new ground had been enclosed with a fence at a cost of £45.

With their improved facilities, the club decided that the time was right to apply for membership of the Scottish Football Association and, in season 1886/87, Thistle participated in the Scottish Cup for the first time.

They were drawn to face Dunfermline in the first round, but Dunfermline were unable to raise a side, and Thistle progressed to round two by way of a 'walk over'.

The second round of the 1886/87 Scottish Cup saw Thistle drawn at home to Cowdenbeath, with whom the honours were shared in a 3-3 draw.

The site of Burntisland Thistle's Lammerlaws Park is now occupied by the Beacon Leisure Centre

Burntisland lodged a complaint to the SFA, however, claiming that their opponents had indulged in "rough and unlawful play", but the governing body rejected the complaint and ruled that the match be replayed as normal and Cowden subsequently progressed to the third round following a 3-1 victory.

As stated previously, Burntisland Thistle failed to negotiate the early rounds of the Fife Cup during their formative years, but all that changed in season 1886/87, when the club reached the final of the highly prestigious tournament for the first time; and an ill-tempered marathon affair it turned out to be!

In the first round, Thistle travelled to Lumphinnans on 18th September 1886, where the home side attempted to oblige their supporters' requests to "go for the man"; jump on him" and "break their legs"!

Burntisland were more than a match for the foul tactics, however, and completely dominated the match, eventually running out victors by seven goals to two. The 'Fifeshire Advertiser' was quick to condemn the antics of the home side, and their report on the match included the following statement:

"For the home team the goalkeeper played well. Of the rest, the less that is said the better, as a coarser, more ignorant set of fellows never entered a football field, their conduct towards the referee – Mr. Love of Clackmannan – being disgraceful, as time after time they threatened to strike him on the field".

The match report, however, so infuriated one Lumphinnans supporter that he felt compelled to write to the 'Fifeshire Advertiser' to vent his frustration as, according to his judgement, there had been "hardly a word of truth" in the newspaper's version of events.

Referring to the paper's opinion that the match had been played in a strong wind, the writer claimed that "there was hardly as much wind as blow the smoke from your pipe". As for the violence meted out by the home players, the correspondent was of the opinion:

"On the change of ends, the play was a little rougher, but the Burntisland team was the first that started it, as one of their players told the Lumphinnans captain that he would punch his heart out"

Sour grapes, or biased reporting on the part of the local press? We shall never know!

In the second round, Thistle were drawn to face Cowdenbeath at home, and a roughly-contested contest ensued at LammerlawsPark on 27th November 1886.

Late in the match, with Burntisland out of sight at four goals ahead, Cowdenbeath resorted to violent conduct which resulted in three Burntisland players bearing the brunt of the visitors' aggressive behaviour.

The match report in the following edition of the 'Fifeshire Advertiser' commented:

"Cowdenbeath's play was something beastly, three of the Thistle's men being injured. First, Webster received a kick in the stomach from Dow, and had to retire for a few minutes. Addison had to leave the field a few minutes before time, and it was thought the Thistle's right-wing was to be deserted entirely, as Philp received a brutal kick in the face from McDonald, but he was able to finish the game."

The semi-final paired Burntisland Thistle with Fife Cup holders Alloa Athletic (Clackmannanshire sides were members of the Fife Association in those days!), and a closely-fought encounter at Alloa's GaberstonPark resulted in a narrow victory for the visitors by two goals to one. Fortunately, this match was played out in a relatively sporting manner!

The final of the Fife Cup, against Dunfermline Athletic on 26th March 1887, was an eagerly anticipated event, with neither side having previously reached the final.

A noisy, boisterous crowd of over 3,000 (a record attendance at that time for a football match in Fife!), crammed in to Ladysmill Park in Dunfermline, where incessant drizzle failed to dampen the enthusiasm of the spectators.

Despite the ball becoming quickly saturated with water, there were chances aplenty at both ends of the park; and, when half-time arrived, Dunfermline held the upper hand due to a hotly-disputed goal.

Fifteen minutes into the second-half, with tempers no doubt frayed due to the conditions, a fight broke out amongst the players after it was alleged that Mackenzie, in the Burntisland goal, had lashed out at a Dunfermline player.

> **GRAND FOOTBALL MATCH**
>
> *FIFESHIRE FOOTBALL ASSOCIATION*
> *FINAL CUP TIE*
>
> # BURNTISLAND THISTLE
>
> V.
>
> # DUNFERMLINE ATHLETIC
>
> at
>
> ## LADY'S MILL PARK, TODAY
> ## (SATURDAY)
>
> Kick-off at 4:15.
>
> *Admission, 6d.; Boys, 3d. Ladies Free.*
>
> Members must Show their Cards at the Gate.
>
> *Refreshments under Grand Stand*

A reproduction of an advertisement for the Fife Cup Final between Burntisland Thistle and Dunfermline Athletic in March 1887

The scene that ensued is perhaps best summed up by the 'Fifeshire Advertiser':

"In an instant all the players were around the goal, and a scene of great confusion followed. Seeing this state of matters, the spectators, who had before this been inside the ropes, rushed into the centre of the field, and joined in what were then real hostilities".

The fighting amongst the crowd and the players escalated and, when intervention by the local police proved fruitless, the referee had no other option but to abandon the game.

The backlash from the law-abiding citizens of the local area was vehement, with some even demanding that the game of football itself be banned as a result of the violent scenes witnesses at Ladysmill!

It was eventually agreed that the match be replayed at the same venue on 16th April 1887 and, when this match finished all-square at a goal-apiece, a third and decisive match was played at Crawford's Park in Cowdenbeath, where Dunfermline Athletic won the trophy for the first time with a 3-1 victory.

The following season, 1887/88, Burntisland Thistle overcame Dunfermline Athletic 4-2 in the first round of the Scottish Cup at Lammerlaws, but this time it was Thistle's turn to be on the receiving end of a protest, with Athletic alleging that the home side had fielded an ineligible player. This time the protest was upheld by the SFA and Burntisland were thrown out of the competition.

Thistle did reach the final of the Fife Cup once again in season 1887/88 but were beaten 6-1 by Lassodie. They eventually resigned from the Fifeshire Football Association in 1889 following a dispute, and their chance of ever landing the Fife Cup was gone.

It was to be season 1890/91 before Burntisland Thistle finally tasted success in the Scottish Cup when they beat Bonnyrigg Rose 4-2 in the first round of the competition on 6th September 1890.

However, scheduled to travel over the newly-opened ForthRailwayBridge to face Heart of Midlothian in the second round on 27th September, Thistle surprisingly scratched from the competition.

Having been thumped 7-0 by Leith Athletic in a "one-sided affair" a week previously, it is perfectly feasible that the club decided to avoid an even greater humiliation at the hands of Scottish League side Hearts!

The following season, 1891/92, Burntisland Thistle made their final appearance in the Scottish Cup, but fell at the first hurdle when they went down by six-goals-to-four to Linlithgow Athletic at LammerlawsPark on 5th September 1891.

The club battled on for a few years, and enjoyed limited success in other cup competitions, including the King Cup and the Edinburgh Shield, but before the end of the nineteenth century Burntisland Thistle had disappeared from the football map.

Senior football is kept alive in the town today through amateur side Burntisland Shipyard, who were founded just after the Great War. Shipyard became members of the Scottish Football Association in 1929 and the Fifeshire Football Association in 1931, thereby establishing themselves as a senior side despite their amateur status. The club have reached the early rounds of the Scottish Cup on a number of occasions, and famously hosted Celtic at their RecreationPark ground in January 1939.

Cameron Bridge F.C.

Football in Fife grew rapidly in popularity during the 1870's and, as that decade neared its end, the game started to take hold in the east of Fife.

The first football club to be founded in the local area was Cameron Bridge F.C., who were established in early 1879. CameronBridge was, as the name might suggest, a club closely associated with the local distillery, and recruited its membership mainly from the workforce; the players being drawn from the manual labourers as well as the white collar staff.

Before long, the club boasted around 25 playing members, with a Mr. G. Gilmour appointed President and Mr. J. A. Gildea appointed Captain, along with T. S. Bailie as secretary and Mr. Houston as treasurer.

The new club were rather fortunate in that the owner of the distillery, Mr. H. V. Haig, was keen to see his employees participate in the sport, and kindly offered the use of part of the extensive grounds of his residence, Cameron House, as a playing field.

The football club gladly accepted the offer, and their first match, played between the members, went ahead on the afternoon of Saturday 8th March 1879. The following extract, taken from the 'East of Fife Record', clearly indicates that the game not only attracted keen interest from those interested in playing the sport, but was also of interest to those who merely wished to watch from the sidelines:

"On Saturday afternoon last, the members of CameronBridge Football Club turned out for the first time and had a few hours pleasant sport in CameronHousePark, kindly granted by Mr. Haig for the use of the club. Many spectators evidently interested in the game were present on the occasion".

It is not known exactly where this football field was laid out within the grounds of Cameron House, but it would almost certainly have been located somewhere on the extensive area of flat land where CameronHospital now sits.

For the remainder of the football season, the members of Cameron Bridge Football Club were happy to play matches amongst themselves at CameronHousePark, but before long the players started to think about laying down a challenge to one of the numerous other football clubs that had become established in Fife at that time. This possibility was also being considered by the 'Fifeshire Advertiser', who, after reporting on the club's progress in mid-April, commented:

"This young club promises well, and by next season we hope to hear of it "holding its own" with any in "ye kingdom"".

In order to better prepare for a match against another club, the members of Cameron Bridge FC organised themselves into two distinct teams from the various departments within the distillery, namely the "Officers and Clerks" and the "Working Men". On Saturday 19th April 1879 the two teams met each other for the first time, and an evenly fought-out contest ended in a draw.

The following month, the two sides played against each other once again, and this time the "Workmen" emerged victorious with a single goal victory, as described in this extract taken from the following edition of the 'Fife Herald':

"The return match of the Officers and Clerks v the Workmen at CameronBridge Distillery came off on Saturday last, and resulted in a victory for the latter by one goal to none. Play commenced at six o'clock, and for the first half-hour was pretty equal, both goals being twice in danger, but the goal-keepers, Ness for the Workmen, and Brown for the Clerks, cleverly saved their respective fortresses. On changing ends at half-time the Workmen forwards came away with a grand rush, and McLean getting a good run passed the ball to Craigie, who scored a goal".

It is rather intriguing that both of the aforementioned matches were low-scoring affairs, as team formations at this time leaned very much towards attack. According to line-ups printed in the press, each side contained a goalkeeper, two full-backs, two half-backs and no fewer than six forwards!

The inaugural season of Cameron Bridge Football Club was wound up with yet another match amongst its members on 7th June 1879, played in front of a good attendance despite wet and windy conditions. The 'Fifeshire Advertiser' commented:

"A pretty stiff eastern breeze blew right across the grounds; while a thick drizzling rain that kept falling almost during the whole time, made it rather unpleasant for the spectators, and the ground was very slippery for the players. The match was, however, a very keenly and evenly contested one, and it is almost wonderful to see the progress this young club has made since its organisation this season. Among the more prominent players, Mr. Gilmour was very noticeable for his all-round good play and grand style of running, while Messrs Ness, Robertson, MacLean, Craigie, Durie and Black were certainly much applauded for some splendid "dribbling"."

Following the match, the club members retired to the Windygates Inn, where they were "entertained to a sumptuous and most substantial dinner"; before the end of the season was commemorated by toasting the club officials and all who had helped to make the team's inaugural season such a success.

The following season, the club's proposal to play a challenge match against another club came off when Burntisland Thistle, one of the top football teams in Fife at the time, visited CameronHousePark on 18th October 1879, and won by five goals without reply.

Further matches then followed, including a return match with Burntisland Thistle on Burntisland Links which ended in a single-goal win for the home side; two heavy defeats from Dunfermline, and a home victory over Markinch Rangers.

A proposed meeting with Edinburgh Caledonian on New-Year's Day 1880 failed to materialise when the Edinburgh side failed to emerge from the train at Cameron Bridge Station!

Unfortunately, interest eventually waned, and Cameron Bridge FC had completely disappeared from the local football scene by the start of the following season. The seeds had been sown in the minds of the local football 'enthusiasts', however, and over the course of the following decade the game of football was destined to become firmly established in the local district!

Kirkcaldy Wanderers

Association football first arrived in Kirkcaldy in 1881. The game of Rugby had been played in the town for some considerable time before this, but the predominantly working class population of the 'Lang Toun' looked upon the oval-ball game as a pastime for the 'toffs', and consequently sought some other form of sports entertainment.

Association football was by now starting to take hold all over Fife, and the working lads of Kirkcaldy reckoned that this sport was more to their liking.

With this in mind, a group of young men decided to pool their resources in order to purchase a football (a rather expensive commodity in the nineteenth century!), before proceeding to play matches amongst themselves on a patch of waste ground adjacent to the town's Maria Street.

Before long, the game of association football had grown so rapidly in popularity with the young men of the 'Lang Toun' that it was decided to form an association football club, and in 1881 Kirkcaldy Wanderers came into being.

The Wanderers wasted no time in making their presence known amongst the established football clubs in Fife and, not long after their formation, they became founder members of the Fifeshire Football Association in 1882 along with Blairadam (Kelty), Burntisland Thistle, Cowdenbeath Rangers, Dunfermline, Dunfermline United, Rossend (Burntisland), St. Leonards (Dunfermline), Vale of Forth (North Queensferry) and Raith Rovers (from Cowdenbeath, NOT the Kirkcaldy version!).

William Jarvis, one of Kirkcaldy Wanderers' star players, who signed for the club from Raith Rovers in 1889.

The new club was extremely fortunate to have a very influential supporter in local councillor Robert Stark, who was also the proprietor of the licenced premises at West Bridge in Linktown, then called the Albion Spirit Vaults, and known today as the Stark's Bar.

Councillor Stark also owned a piece of grazing land at the top of the hill on the west side of the road leading north from his licenced premises, which he kindly allowed the Wanderers to use, free of charge, as their home ground.

The field was then given the name of Stark's Park, the same ground which is today the home of Raith Rovers!

Results during Wanderers' early days were far from impressive, and the new club lost its first five fixtures before eventually tasting success with a six-goal away victory over Edinburgh City Trumpeters.

Gradually, the Wanderers' performances on the field of play started to improve, and before long the club had gained a reputation as a formidable football team, attracting an increasing number of spectators to Stark's Park for home matches.

The club also successfully negotiated reduced rail fares with the North British Railway company for away fixtures!

The game continued to grow in popularity as a participation sport and, in only their second season of operation, the Wanderers were forced to introduce a second and third eleven in order to accommodate the needs of the local budding footballers.

Before long, the Wanderers had established themselves as a club capable of taking on some of the better Scottish football clubs in cup competitions, and in November 1883 the club were draw at home to Heart of Midlothian, who were by then firmly established as a household name, in the first round of the Edinburgh Shield.

Stark's Park was at that time, however, still entirely devoid of any form of pavilion or changing facilities, and the Hearts' players, like every other visiting team, were forced to change in Mr. Stark's licenced premises at the foot of the hill before walking up to the football field!

For the record, despite a brave performance from the home side, the famous Edinburgh club won an entertaining match by three goals to nil.

It was shortly after the Hearts match that the Wanderers' committee realised that if they wanted to establish themselves as a top football club they would have to rectify the situation regarding changing facilities, and subsequently managed to obtain an old club house from Kirkcaldy Golf Club.

The club house was purchased for the princely sum of £10 (a lot of money in those days!) and duly transported to Stark's Park, where it was used for the first time in January 1884.

Anyone familiar with Stark's Park today will be aware that the south-east corner of the playing surface sits high above adjacent Pratt Street. In the 1880's, the playing surface was in roughly the same location, but in those days, with no perimeter fence in place, it was not unheard of for some unfortunate players to lose their footing whilst running down the south-east wing and tumble all the way down to the street below!

This problem was subsequently rectified when the playing surface was roped off; an improvement which also kept the crowd back from the pitch.

When season 1883/84 drew to a close, Wanderers boasted the record of having played eighteen matches, of which twelve had been won and six lost.

The club were of the opinion, however, that more victories should have been recorded, as several goals had not been allowed due to their opponents having claimed, on numerous occasions, that the ball had not passed between the goal posts; there being no such thing as goal nets in those days!

Another drawback with Stark's Park was that it was shared with the local quoiting club, and both football and quoits were often carried out simultaneously. With entry to the quoits being free of charge, the Wanderers found that takings at the gate on match days were not as high as they should have been, as dishonest spectators would simply claim to be attending the quoits match when in actual fact they had come to see the football!

The club continued to grow in stature, but at the end of the 1884/85 season the committee decided that they had outgrown Stark's Park, and decided to look for a new ground that would meet the standards required by an ambitious football team.

The eventual outcome was that Kirkcaldy Wanderers decided to merge with Kirkcaldy Rugby Club, with the intention that the rugby club's home ground at NewtownPark be used for both rugby and association football.

It was also intended that the name 'Wanderers' be dropped, and in future the team would simply be known as Kirkcaldy Football Club. In the event, however, the Wanderers' name continued to be used by both supporters and the local press.

NewtownPark was located adjacent to the railway line at the top end of Nicol Street, where Ava Street and Asquith Street now exist. It was a substantial enclosure with a playing surface that was large enough to accommodate two matches at the same time, and both Wanderers and the rugby club would frequently play simultaneously.

The regular patrons of Newtown Park were, however, more interested in watching the rugby, and initially the Wanderers found that the assembled spectators only turned their attention to the association football match during breaks of play in the oval ball game!

Now based at a properly enclosed venue capable of hosting visits from bigger clubs, the Wanderers successfully applied for membership of the Scottish Football Association, which brought with it entry into the Scottish Cup.

Their first venture into the country's top football competition was a home clash with Dunfermline side Townhill on 1st September 1888, and what was reported to have been a poor game resulted in a 3-0 win for the Wanderers.

Following a bye in the second round, the Kirkcaldy club were handed a home tie with Edinburgh side St Bernard's in round three on 13th October, for which a huge crowd packed into NewtownPark.

The grandstand, which had only recently been erected on the south side of the ground, was reported to be full to overflowing.

A fast and exciting match resulted in a narrow 2-1 victory for the visitors, but controversy surrounded the circumstances leading up to Saints' first goal, as it was alleged that a hand had been used, and the Wanderers exited the competition feeling aggrieved at the outcome.

The following season, the club suffered a humiliating 8-0 reverse at Cowdenbeath in the first round of the Scottish Cup, but in season 1890/91 Wanderers did their reputation no harm at all when they lost narrowly to Hibernian in the first round by the odd-goal-in-seven at Newton Park, where the large contingent of Hibs supporters were reported to have "let themselves be heard very often in not too choice language"!

> **GRAND FOOTBALL MATCHES**
> **AT NEWTON PARK**
>
> NEW YEAR HOLIDAYS
>
> *TUESDAY, 1ˢᵗ January*
> **ROYAL ALBERT**
> (Holders of the Lanarkshire County and Charity Cups;
> Champions of Alliance for 1894)
> v.
> **KIRKCALDY**
> Kick-off at 12 Noon.
>
> *FRIDAY, 4ᵗʰ January*
> **LONDON CASUALS**
> v.
> **KIRKCALDY**
> Kick-off at 2 P.M.
>
> Admission each Match, 6d; Boys, 3d; Ladies free.
> Stand, 6d extra.

A reproduction of a poster advertising football matches at Newton Park in January 1895

In September 1891 the Wanderers played their last-ever match in the Scottish Cup when they lost 3-2 at home to Midlothian side Polton Vale; the club failing to negotiate the qualifying stages of the competition in subsequent years.

As for the Fife Cup, the Wanderers failed to impress despite having been in membership of the Fifeshire Association since its inception, and not once did they progress beyond the semi-final stage.

Various other cup competitions were also entered into, but as far as can be ascertained with limited success.

As for league competitions, Kirkcaldy were members of the original Central League from 1896 to 1898, in which they locked horns with Alloa Athletic, Cowdenbeath, Dunfermline

Athletic, Dundee Reserves, Fair City Athletic (Perth), Hearts of Beath, Lochgelly United and St Johnstone.

The club had earlier competed in the Eastern Alliance against teams from Edinburgh and the Lothians, but dropped out after playing only a handful of matches.

As the nineteenth century drew to a close, it became increasingly apparent that the Wanderers were struggling to stay afloat.

The main reason for the club's demise would appear to have been the rise in prominence of fellow Kirkcaldy club Raith Rovers, who were inaugurated as a junior outfit in 1883 before stepping up to the senior ranks at the start of the 1889/90 season.

Rovers quickly established themselves as the more successful of the town's two senior sides, and the Wanderers' supporters gradually changed their allegiance to their local rivals.

As the 1898/99 season drew to a close, the apathy amongst the Kirkcaldy football public towards the Wanderers was apparent when a crowd of only twenty turned up for a match at NewtownPark, despite the weather being "all that could be desired".

When the situation failed to improve the following season, Kirkcaldy's original senior club decided to call it a day. Shortly after the dawn of the twentieth century, with Kirkcaldy Rugby club having earlier re-located to BeveridgePark, NewtonPark was built over, as previously mentioned, by the houses that now form Ava Street and Asquith Street.

Wemyss F.C.

During the second half of the nineteenth century, coal-mining in the Wemyss district grew rapidly.

With the rapid expansion of the local mining industry, there came a huge influx of miners and their families to the area which, along with the rise in popularity of football throughout the county in the late 1800's, made the introduction of the game to the Wemyss area almost inevitable. This resulted in the formation of Wemyss Association Football Club in 1884.

One major contributory factor to the development of club football in the local district was the improved transport links within the Wemyss area, which allowed teams to travel to neighbouring districts in order to fulfill competition fixtures.

The development of the local railway network can also be directly attributed to the expansion of the mining industry, with the Thornton to Methil branch line, which wound its way through the mines and villages in the Wemyss area, opened as far as Buckhaven in 1881.

The line was subsequently extended as far as the first dock at Methil, which was opened in 1887, in order to cope with the huge amount of coal now being produced and exported from the district, and also to satisfy the demand for passenger services from the main line at Thornton Junction all the way down to Methil via the Wemyss villages and the fishing town of Buckhaven.

Consequently, more football teams were then formed along the course of the railway line around this time, including junior sides Methil Rovers and Buckhaven United.

It is the brief history of senior side Wemyss F.C., however, that is outlined in this chapter.

Wemyss F.C. were based at the intriguingly named FlagpolePark in the village of West Wemyss and, in 1884, the newly-formed club took the bold step of applying to join the recently-founded Fifeshire Football Association, which had been inaugurated only two years previously.

With Kinross and Clackmannanshire clubs having been permitted to join at the beginning of the previous season, the Fifeshire Association boasted no fewer than thirteen members at the beginning of the 1884/85 season. The other teams that would therefore be competing in the Fife Association's prestigious Fife Cup alongside Wemyss F.C. during season 1884/85 were Broomhall (Charlestown), Orwell (Milnathort), Alloa Athletic, Loch Leven Rangers (Kinross), Halbeath, Kingseat, Cowdenbeath, Blairadam (Kelty), Burntisland Thistle, Dunfermline, Kirkcaldy Wanderers and St. Leonard's (Dunfermline).

When the draw was made for the first round of the Fife Cup, at a meeting of the Fifeshire Asociation in Dunfermline on 9th August 1884, the new team was handed an away tie with west-Fife club Kingseat. Unfortunately, Wemyss failed to negotiate the first round of the competition.

The club did continue to play regular matches throughout the 1884/85 season, however, and locked horns with other local clubs including Kirkcaldy AFC, Dunfermline United, Kirkcaldy Star and Kirkcaldy Thistle.

The following season, Wemyss resigned from the Fife Football Association, but continued to play at FlagpolePark under the name Wemyss Blues.

The exact location of FlagpolePark is open to debate, although the writer is of the opinion that he has pinpointed the actual location of the ground with a fair degree of accuracy.

What is known for certain is that the park was in the vicinity of West Wemyss, but due to the non-existence of a piece of ground large enough to contain a football pitch within the village itself, the football ground must have been on the raised land which lies to the north.

As the name would suggest, there must have been a flag pole near to the ground, and Ordnance Survey maps from this period do show a "flag staff" on the raised ground above the 'Lady Pit' and the harbour, although this was surrounded with trees.

On the other side of the main access road into the village, however, opposite the "flag staff", there existed a large area of ground immediately to the rear of the local school, running from west to east, which would have been just big enough to contain a football field.

Match reports at that time do refer to the fact that teams had to occasionally play with a strong wind at their backs which, with the wind prevailing from the west, would mean that Flagpole Park most probably did run in a west-to-east orientation.

The Ordnance Survey maps also indicate that field boundaries, probably hedges, surrounded this particular piece of land. The following extract, taken from a match report which appeared in the 'Fifeshire Advertiser' in October 1886, clearly indicates that the ground was indeed bounded at least in part by a hedge, and must have been enclosed to the extent that an admission fee could be charged:

"a very large number of spectators turned out from the surrounding villages to see the game, making the largest draw at the gate since the football commenced here, although a few young men are still mean enough to line the hedge."

Although the location I have described is only the *probable* location of FlagpolePark, there are actually another two possibilities.

The first is at WemyssCastle, a few hundred metres to the east of the village, where a football tournament was actually held in July 1888.

This tournament, organised as part of an annual fete, was an "invitation" eleven-a-side competition that involved Fife's four top clubs at that time; namely Dunfermline Athletic, Burntisland Thistle, Kirkcaldy Wanderers and Lassodie.

The fact that the grounds of WemyssCastle could accommodate such a tournament would indicate that a substantial football park did exist there, but it is unlikely that such a facility, within the castle grounds, would have been made available for regular football fixtures.

The other possibility is a "football ground" which is depicted on the 1961 Ordnance Survey map located between West Wemyss and Coaltown of Wemyss, but this is also unlikely to be the location of FlagpolePark as this football field would surely have been shown on earlier Ordnance Survey maps had it existed in the 1880's.

Following the demise of the senior club, junior football was played in the village of West Wemyss until at least the end of the nineteenth century, with both Wemyss Athletic and Wemyss United playing at FlagpolePark in the 1890's.
With the development of the village of Coaltown of Wemyss, situated about a mile to the north of West Wemyss, however, football ceased to be played at Flagpole Park, and the football field located to the north of Lochhead Crescent in Coaltown of Wemyss became established as the preferred home ground of local football clubs as the twentieth century progressed.

Lassodie F.C.

The west Fife mining village of Lassodie was developed in the latter half of the nineteenth century when the Lassodie Colliery Company established several pits to the north of Loch Fitty; an area where previously there had existed only Lassodie Mains and Whinnyhall Farms.

Before the end of the century, as well as the aforementioned pits, the village boasted a number of 'miners rows'; a church; a post office; a school; the Lassodie Arms public house; and, last but not least, a football club!

The fact that such a small mining community could support a football club at all is perhaps a little surprising, but the fact of the matter is that Lassodie Football Club not only rose to the status of being a senior club and members of the Fifeshire Football Association; they were also granted full membership of the Scottish Football Association in August 1887, just three years after their formation!

In Lassodie FC's very early days, they played only challenge matches against other local sides, but found the going tough and suffered some hefty defeats, including an 11-1 hammering from Dunfermline at Ladysmill on 13th December 1884.

A year after their formation, at the beginning of the 1885/86 season, Lassodie were admitted to the Fifeshire Football Association; membership of which included participation in the prestigious Fife Cup.

The club didn't exactly set the heather alight during their inaugural season as members of the Fife Association, but all that was to change during season 1886/87, when Lassodie FC made their mark in the Fife Cup and gained a rather unenviable reputation into the bargain!

The Fifeshire Football Association boasted fifteen members at this time and, after having received a bye in the first round of the 1886/87 Fife Cup, Lassodie disposed of near-neighbours Kingseat in round two and were rewarded with a home semi-final against Dunfermline Athletic on 22nd January 1887.

A huge crowd descended on Lassodie's GreenbankPark for the match, with several hundred travelling from Dunfermline to cheer on the Athletic. When the match kicked off at 3:15, the coal-bing adjacent to the ground, which locals referred to as "the grandstand", was fully occupied with noisy, cheering, Lassodie supporters.

Amidst such a hostile atmosphere, it didn't take long for the match to degenerate into a rough and physical encounter, which resulted in Dunfermline's Knight receiving a bad kick on the leg, for which the player was forced to temporarily leave the field. No sooner had the same player returned, he was kicked on the other leg, and had to play out the remainder of the match limping with pain! There was more rough play to come.

Dunfermline Athletic broke the deadlock mid-way through the first half following skilful play down the left-wing and a "well-judged shot" amidst great cheering from the travelling supporters. Rather than attempt to match the skills of their counterparts, however, Lassodie elected to "go for the man rather than the ball", and what resulted was an all-out melee between the players of both sides.

When the second half got under way, the roar from the home supporters perched on the coal-bing was deafening, but rather than inspire their favourites to play more skilful football, the vocal encouragement had the undesired effect that the Lassodie players "piled on the roughness more than ever".

Midway through the second half, Dunfermline's goal-scorer, Sandilands, received a hefty kick in the stomach followed by a punch in the face from Haxton, one of the Lassodie full-backs, and all-hell broke loose.

After the referee had refused the demands of the Dunfermline team that Haxton be ordered off, the Dunfermline captain took his players off the field; all, that is, except for goalkeeper Farquharson, who became involved in a full-blown fist-fight with two of the Lassodie players, who had tried to take advantage of the absence of the rest of the Athletic team by attempting to force the ball into the Dunfermline goal for the equaliser!

The Lassodie club officials then waded in and attacked the Dunfermline goal-keeper; the result of which was that the Dunfermline captain, fearing for the safety of the players, elected not to bring his team back on to the field of play.

Consequently, the match was abandoned, but that wasn't the end of the story. What then followed is best described by this extract taken from the following edition of the 'Dunfermline Saturday Post':

"A general melee ensued, spectators and players engaging in the fight, which lasted for fully an hour. After leaving the field, the crowd continued the brawl in the main street of the village, where they were joined by women, who brandished brooms & c. Had the Lassodie man been put off the field at once this unseemly row might not have occurred"

The feud between the two clubs and their supporters did not end there. Letters were subsequently sent to the 'Dunfermline Saturday Press' from both sides, all claiming that the other club and its supporters were to blame for the fracas.

The editorial staff of the newspaper decided not to print the letters, but instead expressed their opinion on the matter in a rather cryptic way under the heading 'To Correspondents':

"You lay yourself open to the same charge as you prefer against another. Instead of giving the real facts of the case, you seem to have done all in your power to make your statement as incorrect as possible. According to your own showing (although you don't seem to see it), Haxton, one of the Lassodie backs, was the cause of the row".

FIFE CUP TIE.

SEMI - FINAL.

LASSODIE V. DUNFERMLINE ATHLETIC, TO-DAY, at KINGSEAT. Kick-off at 3.30.

Admission, Threepence.

A newspaper advertisement for the Fife Cup Semi-final Replay at Mitchell's Park in Kingseat on 19th February 1887

Once the dust had settled, the match was replayed four weeks later at the neutral venue of Mitchell's Park in nearby Kingseat, where a bumper crowd of over 2,000 assembled to witness the action.

With the weather favourable and the ground in tip-top condition, the conditions were perfect for football, but once again certain Lassodie players let the side down by going for the man instead of the ball; a tactic which brought jeers from the several hundred supporters who had made the trip up from Dunfermline.

The game then degenerated to the same spectacle that had been witnessed on the field of play in the abandoned match, with one player from each side forced to retire, albeit temporarily, after having sustained severe kicks from the opposing side.

With play having been fairly even during the first half, it seemed as if the teams would retire for their half-time cup of tea all square at a goal apiece, but the Athletic had other ideas and forced the ball home to lead 2-1 at the interval.

The second period commenced with play proceeding at a "fast and exciting" pace, and before long Dunfermline scored a third. Lassodie then fell away, allowing the Athletic to take full control, and when the final whistle eventually sounded the Dunfermline side were victors by five goals to one.

Such was the interest in the result of this match, a rather novel method was employed in conveying the score to interested parties back in Dunfermline, as described in the following edition of the 'Dunfermline Saturday Press':

"In view of the interest taken in the match the result was conveyed from the field to Dunfermline by a pair of homer pigeons belonging to Mr. Robert Morris, Forth Street, one of which took only four minutes to cover the distance"

With the Lassodie club having by now built up an unenviable reputation both on and off the field of play, it is perhaps a little surprising that the club successfully applied for full membership of the Scottish Football Association in August 1887, just a matter of months after the disgraceful scenes previously described!

Membership of the SFA, of course, meant that Lassodie would be able to participate in the Scottish Cup competition during season 1887/88, and the club was duly drawn to face Dunfermline Football Club (not Dunfermline Athletic!) at Ladysmill on 3rd September 1887.

With the home team having struggled to raise a side for this match, it was thought that Lassodie would have an easy passage into the second round, and initially the play suggested this would be the case.

Against all the odds, however, Dunfermline emerged victors by three goals to two.

However, it later transpired that the Dunfermline secretary had not submitted his team line to the Scottish Football Association before the set deadline, and Lassodie progressed to the next round of the competition by default!

> SCOTTISH CUP TIE.
>
> GRAND FOOTBALL MATCH.
>
> LASSODIE *V.* DUNFERMLINE at LADY'S MILL PARK TO-DAY.
>
> *Kick-off at* 4 *p.m.   Admission Threepence.*
> Members will receive their Cards at the Gate.

A newspaper advertisement for Lassodie's first-ever Scottish Cup tie, against Dunfermline F.C., which was played at Ladysmill on 3rd September 1887

After receiving a bye in round two, Lassodie were drawn to face Bo'ness at GreenbankPark in the third round, but unfortunately for the Fife team their West Lothian opponents were the better side on the day and emerged victors by three goals to one.

The club did experience success during season 1887/88, however, when they won the Fife Cup at only the third time of asking by thumping Burntisland Thistle by six goals to one in the final at Ladysmill on 21st April 1888, following earlier round victories over Townhill and Kingseat.

The following season saw Lassodie drawn to face Cowdenbeath in the first round of the Scottish Cup at Cowden's then home ground of Mitchell's Park (later known as North End Park), and a keen and evenly fought match was anticipated, although the 'Fifeshire Advertiser' favoured the home side:

"What should cause some stir in the mining villages is the tie between Cowdenbeath and Lassodie. Had the venue of the match been Lassodie, we would not have asked an opinion on who were to be the winners, but seeing the tussle is to take place at Crawford's Park, we think that Cowdenbeath's chances are pretty rosy".

It turned out that the local press predicted correctly, with Cowdenbeath winning the tie by three goals to one.

Season 1889/90 saw Lassodie win a Scottish Cup tie for the first time when they beat Burntisland Thistle 3-2 at home on 7th September 1889. The second round paired the club with Cowdenbeath for the second year in succession, and this time the honours were shared in a 3-3 draw at GreenbankPark.

It was Cowdenbeath, however, who eventually progressed in the competition, when their protest that Lassodie had fielded an ineligible player in the cup-tie was upheld. It transpired that the man in question, Lawson, had turned out for Dunfermline Athletic against Raith Rovers in the first round of the competition, and was therefore "cup-tied"! For the record, Cowdenbeath progressed to the fifth round, where they lost 8-2 to Abercorn.

Subsequent seasons in the country's premier competition proved to be disappointing, with the club never again reaching round two.

The club also reached the Fife Cup Final for a second time in season 1889/90 and again in season 1890/91, but lost on both occasions to Cowdenbeath. They also lost to Raith Rovers in the final of the King Cup in season 1890/91.

In other competitions, Lassodie did have some success in subsequent years, and won the Consolation Cup by beating Edinburgh Adventurers in the final on 7th May 1892 in Dunfermline.

Performances started to deteriorate as the last decade of the nineteenth century progressed, however, and Lassodie were humiliated on several occasions, including a 14-0 thumping at the hands of Raith Rovers and an 8-0 reverse against Kirkcaldy Wanderers.

The writing was on the wall and, following a failed merger with Kingseat to form Loch Rangers in 1894, Lassodie disappeared from the senior football map.

Their ground, Greenbank Park, was completely covered by a pit bing by 1915, and the land where the village of Lassodie once existed has now been entirely swallowed up by the St. Ninians open cast mine workings.

The First Tayport Football Clubs

The earliest association football match that can be traced involving a team from the north-east Fife town of Tayport took place in December 1884, when the second eleven of Monifieth Rangers were reported to have defeated Tayport F.C. by two goals to nil.

Early the following year, a friendly challenge match is reported to have taken place on Tayport Common between Tayport F.C. and a scratch team of locals calling themselves the 'Mussel Dredgers'.

Reporting on the match, the 'Dundee Courier' stated that a large crowd had watched "a fast and exciting game", in which Tayport had emerged victors by two goals to one.

The paper was quick to praise the scratch team, however, stating:

"It is but right to add that the Mussel Dredgers have had only one week's practice. They were heartily applauded for their pluck and perseverance".

The Mussel Dredgers must have enjoyed the experience, because shortly afterwards a new club, Tayport Victoria, was formed by the players who had made up the scratch eleven.

Football in Tayport continued to rise in popularity, and on 30th March 1885 the Courier reported that another new club, Our Boys, had been founded.

This team was closely associated with the Tayport Spinning Company, which had contributed generously towards the cost of setting up the club.

The earliest match that can be traced involving Our Boys was a 3-0 home defeat to Taymouth of Broughty Ferry on Saturday 18th April 1885, and records would suggest that this was the only match they played during the 1884/85 season.

The following season, however, Our Boys played regularly, and recorded some impressive wins, including a 4-2 local derby victory over Tayport and a 5-0 thrashing of Dundee Central.

With football continuing to rise in popularity in the Tayport area, more new clubs were started, and during the course of the 1885/86 season there was no fewer than five teams based in the town; namely Our Boys, Tayport F.C., Tayport Victoria, Craigmount and Tayport Wanderers.

Before the end of the season, however, Our Boys had firmly established themselves as the foremost team in Tayport and, following victories over Dundee Camperdown and Dundee Alert, rounded off their campaign with a seven-nil drubbing of the intriguingly named Broughty Bakers on 5th May.

Our Boys now considered themselves capable of taking on the best teams in Fife, and duly applied for membership of the Fifeshire Football Association, to which they were admitted at the beginning of the 1886/87 season.

At a meeting of the Fife Association, held in the Blyth Hotel in Dunfermline on Saturday 14th August 1886, it was reported that there were now fifteen clubs in the Association's membership; the other clubs being Alloa Athletic, Alloa United, Burntisland Thistle, Clackmannan, Cowdenbeath, Dunfermline, Dunfermline Athletic, Kingseat, Kirkcaldy Wanderers, Lassodie, Lumphinnans, Strathforth (Inverkeithing), Townhill and Vale of Forth (Alloa).

The draw for the first round of the Fife Cup was made at the meeting, and Our Boys' name came out of the hat paired with Cowdenbeath, one of the County's top teams and Fife Cup finalists the previous season.

The eagerly awaited Fife Cup tie was played at Crawford's Park in Cowdenbeath (later to become North End Park) on Saturday 11th September 1886, where the competition's newcomers suffered a heavy defeat in what was their first-ever competitive fixture, with the 'Fife Free Press' reporting:

"FIFESHIRE CUP TIE, COWDENBEATH v OUR BOYS, TAYPORT – Our Boys journeyed to Cowdenbeath on Saturday afternoon for the purpose of playing off their tie for the Fifeshire Cup. After a good game the Cowdenbeath team were declared to be the victors by six goals to nil"

Our Boys were not too disheartened, however, and proceeded with plans to establish a more permanent football ground on which to play home matches.

At the statutory annual meeting of the Feuars and Inhabitants of Tayport, held in the Temperance Hall on Monday 27th September 1886, a letter was read from the secretary of Our Boys Football Club asking permission to erect permanent goal posts on Tayport Common. The request was granted, and it looked like the club now had a firm foundation on which to build!

Unfortunately, the team then lost some key players who had moved out of the town, which resulted in Our Boys suffering some heavy defeats towards the end of the year, including a ten-nil hammering from Dundee namesakes Our Boys Rangers at WestCraigiePark on 11th December 1886. Two of the other Tayport clubs were experiencing the same difficulty regarding players, and in January 1887 the decision was taken to amalgamate Our Boys with Tayport F.C. and Craigmount.

The 'Dundee Courier', on 31st January, commented:

"TAYPORT – Owing to several members of the three clubs leaving the place, it was thought advisable to amalgamate so as to form one good club. This has been done, and it is now named the Abertay. Their opening match was played on Saturday against the Star of Eden (Guardbridge). The Abertay won by seven to nil".

The new club followed up their inaugural victory with a convincing win over Dundee Ancients by six goals to one at the beginning of February 1887, but later that same month disaster struck when Dundee's Our Boys Rangers hammered Abertay by SEVENTEEN goals without reply!

The performance really was as one-sided as the score-line suggests, with the 'Dundee Courier' commenting:

"The game partook of the nature of a fiasco, there being really only one team in it".

Undaunted, Abertay carried on and managed to secure a number of victories before the end of the season, which gave the club officials sufficient confidence to apply for membership of the Fifeshire Football Association. This was granted at the beginning of the 1887/88 season and, in the first round of the Fife Cup, Abertay were drawn to face 'big-guns' Burntisland Thistle at Lammerlaws Park.

No trace of this match can be found, however, and we must assume that Abertay scratched from the competition for reasons unknown. Although there were some further matches played by the club, Abertay had disappeared from the football map before the end of the 1887/88 season, and Tayport bade farewell to senior football.

The other aforementioned clubs had also been wound up by this time, but the association game was subsequently resurrected in the town with the formation of several other clubs, and the game is kept well and truly alive today through the highly successful Tayport Juniors football club.

Star of Leven and Vale of Leven

The first organised football clubs in the town of Leven were Star of Leven and Vale of Leven, both of which were founded in or around 1885, and both of which existed almost simultaneously until 1889. For this reason, the history of both clubs has been combined into one chapter.

The writer would like to make it clear, at this stage, that neither club had any connection whatsoever with the Dunbartonshire clubs of the same name that featured in the very early years of the Scottish Cup!

During their entire existence, neither club played in any competition, and their fixture lists comprised of only friendly challenge matches or charity encounters against other Fife clubs of a similar standing.

The two Leven clubs did play each other on numerous occasions, however; the first such encounter having taken place over two legs in early 1886, with the following press report on the second meeting, which appeared in the 'Fife Herald' on Wednesday 10th February 1886, indicating that the game of football was rapidly gaining popularity in the town:

"On Saturday the opening return match between Vale of Leven and Star of Leven clubs came off on the ground of the latter. After a long, keen struggle, the match was declared drawn. A large number of people turned out to see the match. The game appears to gain popularity here every day".

The game was also gaining in popularity throughout the east of Fife at the time, and Star of Leven were popular visitors to the East Neuk, where they played Anstruther Rovers on numerous occasions on "the cricket field" at Rodger Street in Cellardyke, as well as Cellardyke Bluejackets, who shared the same home ground.

Such was the interest in one such fixture, played against Anstruther Rovers at Rodger Street on Saturday 6th March 1886, that a crowd of over 500 turned out to witness the event. Later that same year, a similar attendance assembled at the same venue for a visit from the Star, only to be disappointed by the non-appearance of the Leven team; no doubt lack of communication being largely to blame (the telecommunications we take for granted today simply didn't exist in 1886!).

Vale of Leven, on the other hand, preferred to travel to the west of Fife to fulfill their fixtures, and regularly played clubs such as Lochgelly Athletic, Kirkcaldy Union and Cowdenbeath St Leonard's.

Both Star and Vale, of course, played regular home fixtures against all the aforementioned teams and also against other local clubs including Methil Rangers, Dysart, Vale of Eden (Cupar), White Cross (Guardbridge), Giffen Park (Dysart), Crail Union, Kirkcaldy Albion and Burntisland N.B. (who were presumably a club associated with the North British Railway Company).

Some of these clubs, notably the teams from the west of Fife, considered Leven an attractive destination and venue for their sport. Occasionally, as is apparent from the following extraction taken from the 'Fifeshire Advertiser' in May 1886 (referring to a match between Star of Leven and Kirkcaldy Albion), the visiting players made the most of their day out:

"The Albion closed their season on Saturday with a drive to Leven, where they played a friendly game with the Star of that town. In the first half the Albion scored three goals, and in the second half the Star had one goal – the match thus resulting in a win for the Albion by three goals to one. After spending an hour in a social manner with the Leven team, the Albion adjourned to the Shorehead, where, along with the lads and lassies of Leven, they tripped the light fantastic toe to the enlivening strains of Lundin Mill Brass Band".

The subject of home fixtures raises the question of where Star and Vale played their home games? Unfortunately, this is not well documented, but what we know for certain is that Star of Leven, from at least March 1887, played in a field belonging to a Mr. Young of Burnmill.

A study of early Ordnance Survey maps would suggest that the only piece of flat ground large enough to accommodate a football field in the vicinity of Burnmill is the land now occupied by Balfour's foundry on the south side of Leven Vale.

Vale of Leven, on the other hand, are known to have played their home matches mainly at the 'Haugh House', which research has concluded must have existed on the western side of the present-day Mountfleurie housing estate, sandwiched between Shepherd Avenue and the local supermarket.

Throughout their existence, of course, both Star and Vale continued to play regular matches against each other and, although the initial meetings between the two clubs back in early 1886 appear to have been played in the best of spirits, as time went by fierce rivalry grew between the pair, and eventually it became apparent that there was no love lost between the sides!

In March 1887, an argument broke out when Vale's late equaliser against Star was disallowed, which resulted in the match being abandoned when the Vale team refused to take any further part in the proceedings.

Then, in October of the same year, rough play ensued during a charity match at the Haugh House between Star and Vale, which had been arranged (rather ironically!) to raise funds for a Vale player who had been unable to work after having been injured earlier in the season.

In front of a large crowd, the players proceeded to kick lumps out of each other, and the "action" is perhaps best described by this extract taken from the 'Fifeshire Advertiser':

"The match was one of the roughest ever seen played, and a disgrace to the teams. The Vale are a very heavy team, and are not afraid to put their weight on the man instead of the ball".

This was not a view held by one angry spectator, however, who wrote to the same paper to complain about the rough play meted out by the Star!

In May 1889 rough play once again ensued in the "local derby", and this time it was a Star supporter who felt compelled to contact the local press, resulting in the following comment being printed in the 'Fifeshire Advertiser':

"A spectator, who has not sent his name, accuses the Vale players of being rough, alleging that one of them jumped on the Star goalkeeper while he was down on the ground, and also that after the match the Star received shabby treatment at the hands of their opponents".

Both Star of Leven and Vale of Leven folded in 1889, around the same time that Leven F.C., the first Senior club to play in the Levenmouth area, was founded. Unfortunately, this club also gained a reputation for rough play, and folded shortly after losing to Burntisland Thistle in the 1889/90 Fife Cup.

The name Star of Leven was resurrected in 1893 when a junior team of that name was founded, but this club had no connection with its predecessor.

Strathforth F.C.

The building of the ForthRailwayBridge, which lasted from 1882 until 1890, was a labour-intensive project which also involved the construction of tunnels, cuttings and embankments.

The population of the towns and villages surrounding the new bridge increased temporarily as a direct result of the scheme, due to the huge influx of engineers and navvies to the area.

With association football starting to take a grip on Fife at this time, especially in the western part of the county, it was inevitable that the game would take hold in the areas where the temporary workforce had taken up residence, which resulted in Strathforth Football Club being established during the mid-1880's.

Strathforth F.C. were founded in or about 1885, and were based at Ballast Bank in Inverkeithing. By early 1886, the club had become well enough established to operate two teams, who played simultaneously on Saturday afternoons; one at home and the other away.

It was during 1886 that the Strathforth committee considered their club capable of competing with the best teams in Fife, and duly applied for membership of the Fifeshire Football Association, to which they were admitted at the beginning of the 1886/87 season along with fellow newcomers Alloa United, Tayport Our Boys, Townhill and Clackmannan.

The Fifeshire Association now boasted a record fifteen clubs; the other members being Alloa Athletic, Burntisland Thistle, Cowdenbeath, Dunfermline, Dunfermline Athletic, Kingseat, Kirkcaldy Wanderers, Lassodie, Lumphinnans and Vale of Forth (Alloa).

The site of Strathforth F.C.'s Ballast Bank ground, which was located adjacent to Preston Crescent in Inverkeithing. It is still open ground today, and is used for youth football.

In the Fife Cup, Strathforth knocked out fellow new-boys Townhill in the first round, and were rewarded with a second-round tie against Dunfermline Athletic at East EndPark, where the Inverkeithing side went down by four goals without reply.

Strathforth lodged a complaint to the Fifeshire Association following this game, however, in which certain objections to the condition of East EndPark were raised, along with an allegation of "rough play" by their opponents. At a subsequent meeting of the Association, the complaint was "dismissed in consequence of informality and lodgement".

Strathforth did, however, record some impressive results during their inaugural season as a senior club, and hammered Kirkcaldy Wanderers, then one of the county's top sides, by six goals without reply at Ballast Bank on 27th November 1886.

Reporting on the match, the Kirkcaldy-based 'Fife Free Press' commented:

"The Wanderers received a complete dusting from the Strathforth", before concluding: *"really, Wanderers, you must pull up!"*

Early the following year, Strathforth overcame another top Fife club, Cowdenbeath, by a single goal at Ballast Bank, in what was reported to have been "a hard and fast game".

Towards the end of the 1886/87 season, proof of the involvement of railway bridge construction workers in local football was confirmed by a match report which appeared in the 'Dunfermline Saturday Press' on 30th April 1887:

"On Saturday, a match took place between two Inverkeithing teams, the Strathforth and the Strollers, on the Ballast Bank of the town. There was a good turnout of spectators, the inducement no doubt being to see the first match played by the Strollers, a team composed of Dundee and Glasgow men, chiefly workmen at the Forth Bridge."

For the record, Strathforth emerged victors by three goals to one.

As well as retaining membership of the Fifeshire Association for season 1887/88, Strathforth successfully applied for membership of the Edinburgh Football Association, which allowed the club to participate in the Edinburgh Shield and the King Cup; both prestigious competitions at the time.

In the latter competition, the club found themselves paired once again with Townhill, and the subsequent report on this cup-tie, which appeared in the 'Dunfermline Saturday Press' on 19th November 1887, contained the following lines, which seem rather amusing by today's standards:

"With about twenty minutes to play, Bathgate, for the Townhill, forced both goalkeeper and ball through the posts, but for some unknown reason, the referee refused to give a goal".

In the Fife Cup, Strathforth were knocked out by Blairadam in a first round replay following an exciting 5-5 draw at Ballast Bank.

In season 1888/89, Strathforth again featured in the draw for the second round of the Fife Cup, but only because they received a bye in the first round. The Inverkeithing side came out of the hat paired with the Fife Association's newest club, Lochgelly Athletic, with the tie scheduled to take place at CooperhallPark, Lochgelly, on 1st December 1888.

A rather one-sided match resulted in an absolute hammering for Strathforth, who were soundly beaten by an in-form Lochgelly Athletic by eleven goals to one!

This humiliation appears to have completely knocked the heart out of the Inverkeithing club, who subsequently decided to withdraw from the Fifeshire Football Association.

No further reference to Strathforth Football Club can be found after this date, and we must therefore assume that the club was wound up in 1889; thus ending the town of Inverkeithing's brief flirtation with the senior game.

There is evidence to suggest that a junior team of the same name was founded in or around 1894, but like its forebears this club enjoyed only a very brief existence.

Vale of Eden

The 'County Town' of Cupar, which was Fife's main administration centre from the 13th Century until Glenrothes took over that role in 1970's, was comparatively late in arriving on the association football scene.

Like its near neighbour St. Andrews, the game of rugby was the main winter team sport played in Cupar from the early 1870's, with cricket being extremely popular in the summer months.

Cupar Rugby Club, established in 1874, played on a ground on the west side of Castlebank Road, which is now built over by the Braehead housing scheme.

The cricket club played at BonvilPark, which was located on the north side of the main road west to Auchtermuchty, and it was the transformation of BonvilPark into a public park that ultimately brought about the establishment of association football in Cupar.

It was in the early 1880's that the idea of forming a public park for the town, which was to incorporate improved facilities for the cricket club along with lawn tennis courts and other amenities, was first mooted. The idea quickly gained popularity amongst the local population, and a series of fund-raising events was organised in order to raise funds, with the dream eventually becoming a reality in 1885.

It didn't take long for the success of the venture to receive the approval of the local press, with the 'Fife Herald' commenting:

"The laying out of BonvilPark as a Cricket and Lawn Tennis ground may do more for Cupar than one would at first suppose. It has afforded many pleasant hours recreation to the lovers of these excellent games".

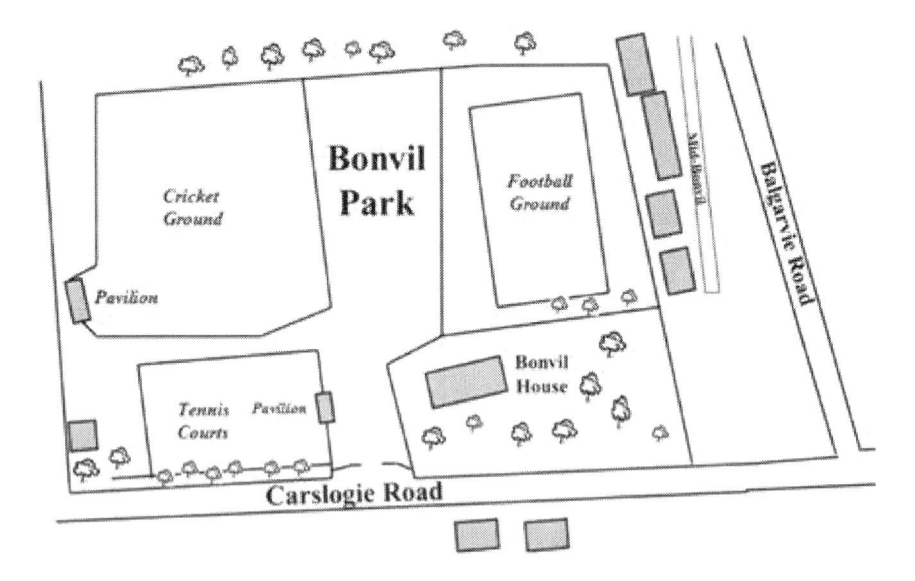

Bonvil Park in the late nineteenth century, showing the location of Vale of Eden's football ground. The park is now known as DuffusPark, and the football pitch has now been rotated ninety degrees to lie in an east-west orientation. The cricket field is now occupied by the Howe of Fife rugby ground.

The Herald went on to say how the new improved facility had attracted large numbers of spectators, both from the town and the outlying villages, which had imparted *"an activity and gaiety to our thoroughfares that is quite enlivening"*.

It was inevitable then, when the cricket and tennis seasons came to an end, that the sports enthusiasts of the town would be keen to make use of Bonvil Park during the winter months, and Vale of Eden football club (not to be confused with a Dundee club of the same name which was extant in the mid to late 1880's) came into existence at the beginning of the 1885/86 season.

The football pitch was laid out on the eastern part of BonvilPark, with the cricket ground occupying the western part and the tennis courts located to the south.

The first match played by Vale of Eden was on 10th October 1885, when local side Blebo, from Dura Den, visited Cupar and defeated the new club by four goals-to-nil.

It didn't take long for the Vale to become established in local football circles, however, and in January 1886 the Cupar team fought out a very creditable one-all draw with Star of Leven, in which "some splendid pay was witnessed".

Before the end of their inaugural season, the Vale were attracting sizeable crowds to their home games, even in inclement weather conditions.

On 6th February 1886, Vale played host to Raith Rovers, where an "enjoyable match" was witnessed, despite the fact that the frozen spectators had to suffer a 4-0 defeat for the home side on a BonvilPark playing surface that was inches deep in snow!

Overall, it has to be said that results were not favourable during the early days, and Vale suffered some heavy defeats, especially against local rivals Tayport.

On one occasion, in a match against Anstruther Rovers, when at last the Cupar side looked to be heading for a possible one-nil victory, the match was abandoned with just minutes remaining when fighting broke out amongst the players!

Vale continued to struggle throughout the following season and suffered some heavy defeats, including a 7-1 hammering from the second eleven of Broughty Football Club and a 9-0 home thumping from Raith Rovers.

Regular visitors to Bonvil Park in the late 1880's were Star of Leven, who always made the relatively short journey north from the coastal town by horse and cart; there being no direct rail link between Leven and Cupar.

The matches between Vale of Eden and Star of Leven were always closely-fought affairs which attracted large crowds, and it was against the Star that Vale recorded some of the few victories enjoyed by the club.

Unfortunately, performances failed to improve as the seasons progressed, and eventually interest in the game of association football in the Fife county town waned.

The last match involving Vale of Eden that can be traced took place in October 1888, and it would appear that the club folded shortly after this, with Cupar once again reverting to its previous status of being a rugby and cricket town, albeit for a relatively short period.

Following unsuccessful efforts in 1889 to form a football team associated with the local cricket club, an association football club was eventually established once again in Cupar late in 1891, when a group of local printers got together to form Thane of Fife football club.

Cupar Athletic, a junior club that occasionally flirted with the senior game, was also founded around the same time.

The Vale of Eden name lived on in Fife football circles, however, with clubs of that name existing in Ladybank, Auchtermuchty and Guardbridge during the 1890's.

BonvilPark was eventually re-named DuffusPark, and is today home to both Cupar Hearts F.C. and Howe of Fife rugby club.

The football pitch is in the same location within the park as it was during the 1880's, but now runs from east to west as opposed to its original orientation of north to south.

The First Kirkcaldy Junior Clubs

The first association football club to be founded in the 'Lang Toun' was Kirkcaldy Wanderers in 1881; the history of which was detailed in an earlier chapter.

The formation of the Wanderers sparked an immediate increase of the popularity of the game in Kirkcaldy and, within a few years, several junior clubs had been established, including the Albion, the Thistle, the Union, Raith Rovers, the Rangers, Pathhead United, the Ramblers, the Star, and Blackburn.

Unlike today, when an abundance of public parks exists in Kirkcaldy and beyond to facilitate the needs of the local teams, a distinct lack of playing facilities in the late 1800's meant that the local football clubs were constantly searching for suitable places to play the game.

In an article which appeared in the 'Fifeshire Advertiser' in 1913, reminiscing about the roots of the game in Kirkcaldy, the problems endured by clubs in securing suitable grounds in the early days is portrayed:

"These clubs led a very uncertain and precarious existence, and were continually on the hunt for playing pitches and for players. When a group of youths had scraped together as much as purchase the coveted "fitba", they had to learn their football either on the sands when the tide was out or on some very rough ground indeed. In the former case a team's defence was more liable to be blinded by sand scooped in their eyes by an opponent's foot rather than the brilliance of the legitimate footwork. Those clubs which were fortunate enough to secure the use of a stubble field from some local farmer considered themselves on a much higher plane than their rivals on the sands, but their tenure of occupancy was not so very much more secure than that of those who were ruled by the flowing of the tide".

Scott Brown, a stalwart for Kirkcaldy Albion during the 1880's.

The most successful of the aforementioned junior clubs were Kirkcaldy Albion and Raith Rovers, both founded in 1883.

Both clubs had the luxury of having tenancy of a ground on which to play, which no doubt contributed to their success; Albion at Elder's Park near Bogie Farm and Raith at Robbie's Park, where BeveridgePark exists today.

For several seasons these two clubs in particular were fierce rivals, and regularly faced each other in the latter stages of the local cup competitions.

There was also no love lost between Albion and Kirkcaldy Thistle, and the pair fought out a series of ill-tempered matches in the final of a "Badge Competition" in March 1885.

> GRAND FOOTBALL MATCH. — UNDECIDED BADGE TIE.—THISTLE v. ALBION TO-DAY (SATURDAY), 28th March, in STARK'S PARK. Kick-off at 3.30 p.m. Admission, 2d; Boys, 1d; Ladies Free. After expenses, proceeds will be handed over to Unemployed Fund.

A newspaper advertisement for the Thistle v Union "Badge Competition" match at Stark's Park on 28th March 1885

In the first meeting between the sides, played on "Mr. Stark's field", the Albion emerged victorious by the odd-goal-in-five, but their joy was short-lived.

Thistle's protest that the winners had fielded an ineligible player was upheld, and so the cup final was replayed at the same venue three weeks later, before *"the largest number of spectators that ever assembled to witness a football match in Kirkcaldy"*.

After this match ended all-square, both teams returned to Stark's Park on 28th March 1885, where a fiercely fought battle ensued.

Albion kicked off, and almost immediately started to pressurize the Thistle goal. The match was only minutes old when their dominance paid off and the opener was scored to the delight of their followers; the goal and subsequent celebrations being vividly described in the report which appeared in the following edition of the 'Fifeshire Advertiser':

"The right wing, running away and getting past the backs, centred to Connolly, who gave the ball the finishing touch, sending it between the posts amid loud cheers".

After the re-start, the game stepped up a gear as Thistle fought hard for the equaliser, but unfortunately the match degenerated somewhat, and an element of rough play crept in; the foul play actually being encouraged by the large vociferous crowd, as is evident from the match report:

"On kicking off the play began to get faster, a lot of the rough element being indulged in by both teams, urged on, no doubt, by their respective followers".

During the second half, following an incident in front of goal, the Thistle team walked off the park in protest, but were eventually persuaded to return ten minutes later. For the record, Albion held on to their single goal advantage.

It was Raith Rovers who ultimately established themselves as the most successful Kirkcaldy junior club, however, and eventually considered themselves good enough to step up to the senior ranks, which they did in 1889, thus becoming the town's second senior outfit alongside Kirkcaldy Wanderers.

Raith did, however, maintain a presence in junior football circles at that time with the formation of Raith Athletic, who competed in various competitions, including the West Fife Junior League, until they ceased operations in 1906.

Several junior clubs continued to operate in Kirkcaldy alongside the senior clubs, but there was a general opinion expressed in the media that there were too many teams in the town, both junior and senior, and that amalgamation might be the best way forward, not just to form one strong team, but to pool resources in order to secure the tenancy of a football ground befitting a successful football club.

Raith Rovers, pictured with the Kirkcaldy Cup just before the club stepped up to the senior ranks in 1889.

One example quoted was that of fellow Fife club Dunfermline Athletic, who held an enviable position according to the 'Fifeshire Advertiser' in December 1889:

"There is no opposition, and they have a fine ground, which ought to tempt the young fellows to play. Several of the Kirkcaldy teams wish they had the same chance to prosper. If the whole of the football clubs in Kirkcaldy were merged into one club like the Athletic, they would have plenty of players for one thing. It is a wonder how so many of them succeed here".

As for the facilities enjoyed by the west Fife club, the same newspaper commented:

"The Athletic have a fine enclosure at Dunfermline now. The Dyke which runs along the south side of the park has been topped with a wooden barricade, and completely shuts out the view from the road".

Of course, the scenario prophesised by the 'Fifeshire Advertiser' in the late nineteenth century eventually came to pass, with Raith Rovers being the only club to survive.

All of the other junior clubs referred to in this chapter ceased operations before the dawn of the twentieth century, although the names of some of the clubs, including Albion and Thistle, were resurrected in later years.

Cellardyke Bluejackets

Association football first arrived in the east of Fife fishing village of Cellardyke in September 1885 with the formation of the Anstruther and Cellardyke Association Football Club.

Football fever then took hold on the community and, before long, the village boasted a second club; the intriguingly named Maggie Lauder F.C., which shared its name with the local cricket club. This club was so called, it is presumed, in tribute to a popular nineteenth century folk song of the same name about a beautiful young Cellardyke lass!

Maggie Lauder F.C. played matches regularly within the confines of the local area, and included amongst their opponents the equally intriguingly named Anstruther clubs Rob Roy F.C. and Radicals F.C.

By June 1886, Maggie Lauder F.C. had disappeared from the local football scene to be replaced by Cellardyke Bluejackets, a football club founded by the local fishermen.

Such was the nature of the fishing occupation, however, that the club members' free time was dictated not just by the state of the tide, but by the fact that the fishing boats could be away from home for some considerable and unpredictable time, which meant that playing regular fixtures against other clubs and participating in organised competitions was out of the question!

The Bluejackets, therefore, initially played only matches arranged amongst their members as and when their occupation allowed.

A Cellardyke Bluejackets player dressed in typical nineteenth century football kit

On 19th February 1887, however, the Bluejackets did finally manage to arrange a match against Anstruther Rovers, which they lost by two goals to nil. Exactly four weeks later the two clubs played a "return match", in which Cellardyke Bluejackets recorded their first-ever victory with a two-nil win.

Organised games continued to be few and far between, and the next organised match played by the club came almost a year later, in January 1888, when the "Blues" lost a challenge match to Crail Union Reserves by three goals without reply.

Further heavy defeats were to follow, but eventually the Bluejackets were confident enough to challenge clubs from outside the East Neuk of Fife and, on 27th April 1889, recorded an impressive single-goal victory over Star of Leven in Cellardyke.

The club was by now coming to the attention of the local press and, in an article previewing the new football season which appeared in the 'East of Fife Record' in September 1889, Cellardyke Bluejackets were listed as the third-best club in the local area behind Crail Union and Anstruther Rangers.

The club still drew their players from the local fishing community, however, and the same article lamented the fact that the Bluejackets did not play on a regular basis due to the fact their players were all engaged at the fishing, quite often some distance from home, and therefore not in a position where regular matches could be organised.

The point was made, though, that the Cellardyke team had frequently played matches when fishing "in the South of England" (probably Lowestoft or Yarmouth), and were therefore the most travelled club in the district!

The Martin White Cup was a handsome silver trophy, introduced in 1893, to be competed for by football clubs in the St. Andrews group of burghs; including those clubs hailing from Cupar, St Andrews, Crail, Cellardyke, Anstruther and Pittenweem.

Because of their circumstances, it was not possible for the Bluejackets to participate in any league competition, and when the East of Fife Football League was inaugurated in December 1892 the Cellardyke club was unable to enter.

However, early in 1893, it was announced that a knock-out cup competition, the Martin White Cup, was to be introduced to the east of Fife, and there was a distinct possibility that the "Blues" could well participate.

The following article, relating to the new tournament, appeared in the 'Dundee Evening Telegraph' on 11th May 1893:

"TROPHY FOR CLUBS IN ST. ANDREWS BURGHS – Mr. J. Martin White of Balruddery has given a handsome silver trophy to be competed for by the football clubs in the St Andrews group of burghs. These will include the clubs in Cupar, St Andrews, Crail, Cellardyke, Anstruther and Pittenweem."

The Bluejackets duly made their mark on the competition over the course of the following seasons and eventually, in April 1903, the club's finest hour finally arrived when both they and local rivals Anstruther Rangers reached the final of what had become one of the most prestigious tournaments in the east of Fife.

The Rangers were expected to win easily, especially as they had ground advantage, but the "Blues" had other ideas and, following a closely fought first forty-five minutes, took control during the second half and deservedly ran out winners by two-goals-to-one.

It was an unexpected outcome, but one which was welcomed throughout the close-knit fishing community of Cellardyke, as their team had, against all the odds, managed to "get one over" their more fancied local rivals.

Cellardyke Bluejackets with the Martin White Cup in 1903

The local 'East of Fife Record' commented:

"It would be pretty hard to say which was the most surprised team of the two, the Blues for their unexpected and entirely deserved win, or their opponents at their defeat from a team against which they always thought they could go one better".

Cellardyke Bluejackets continued to play for a number of seasons after their famous cup win and were certainly still in existence in February 1907, when records state they were forced to scratch from a Martin White Cup tie against St. Andrews City, presumably for reasons connected with the fishing industry!

There is no trace of the club in later years, although a team of the same name did play in the North East Fife Sunday Amateur League during season 1992/93.

Crail Union

Crail Union, the most easterly-based football club to have existed in the Kingdom of Fife, was founded in 1886, shortly after the first East Neuk of Fife football club, the Anstruther and Cellardyke Association Football Club, was founded in 1885.

The first recorded match played by Crail Union that can be traced with any certainty was a home meeting with Anstruther Swifts (who were the second eleven of Anstruther Rovers; the club that arose from the ashes of the short-lived Anstruther and Cellardyke AFC) on 2nd October 1886. The match was not one the 'Crailers' would care to remember, however, with the Anstruther second string winning by five goals without reply; a result which would do little to instill confidence for the future!

However, within a very short period, the new team's form improved dramatically and, early the following year, the Union proved that they were able to hold their own against Anstruther Rovers' first eleven; a meeting between the two sides in Crail on 22nd January 1887 resulting in a draw of one goal each. Playing a brilliant match at centre-forward for Crail that afternoon was Morris, a player who had previously seen service with Heart of Midlothian, which should give a fair indication of the quality of player now pulling on the Union jersey!

Crail Union went from strength to strength over the following seasons, and eventually established themselves as the top football club in the East Neuk of Fife, regularly beating local rivals Anstruther Rovers, Cellardyke Bluejackets, Anstruther Rangers, Pittenweem and Elie Thistle. The club also became well respected in other parts of Fife and even further a-field, with regular opponents including high-standing clubs such as Pathhead United (Kirkcaldy), Kirkcaldy United, Kirkcaldy

Albion, Lochgelly, and even the much-renowned Dundee club Strathmore. In fact, it is claimed that Crail Union remained unbeaten at home for over two years from early in 1887 until Kirkcaldy United won 5-3 in Crail on 4th May 1889!

The Union's matches were always fiercely contested, which inevitably resulted in on-field arguments and fall-outs between the players. There are two matches, played towards the end of 1888, when this discord was well documented in the pages of the local press.

The first instance, reported in the 'Fifeshire Advertiser', occurred on Saturday 17th November at WaidPark in Anstruther, towards the end of a match with Anstruther Rangers. Playing with a gale-force wind at their backs, the Union were a goal to the good when the half-time whistle sounded. During the second half, however, the Rangers used the conditions to their advantage and soon turned the game around, despite the Union's best efforts to keep the score respectable by fair or foul means! The following extract, taken from the 'Fifeshire Advertiser' on 23rd November 1888, gives a fair indication of how tempers became frayed as the match progressed due to Crail adopting unsporting tactics:

"From a throw-in near the Union's goal, the ball was headed in and a goal was certain had not Henderson, one of Union's backs, fisted it out. A scrimmage ensued but was cleared. The ball being returned, the Rangers centre shot it into the goalkeeper's hands, and he in trying to save stepped fully two feet behind the bar, the ball of course being through. This caused a lot of wrangling, and the Union left the field before full time. Result: Rangers 4 goals; Union 1 goal".

Just weeks later, on 29th December, a similar situation arose in a home match against Cellardyke Bluejackets, which ended with the Cellardyke team walking off, as was reported in the following edition of the 'Fife Herald':

"Play began briskly at 3 o'clock, and in a quarter-of-an-hour the Blue Jackets scored a scrimmage goal. The ball was across the line, but the Union team forced it back. This led to a hot discussion, which ended in the Blue Jackets indignantly leaving the field".

Fortunately, the reputation of Crail Union which spread throughout the football world was of the positive variety and, in February 1889, a letter praising the club appeared in the 'Scottish Sport' newspaper. The letter was, admittedly, from "an esteemed correspondent from Crail, Fifeshire", but if the contents were to be believed then the reputation of the letter-writer's local football team had certainly made its mark in the higher echelons of the game:

"As I am a reader of your athletic paper (Sport), and as I wish to show you what rapid strides football is taking in the 'East Neuk o' Fife', I hope you will allow me space for this note. To begin with, I may mention that the worthy match secretary of the Crail Union had a note today, bearing the London post-mark, wishing him to arrange a date for a home and home match with the Preston North End. This is not the only challenge match the now famous Crail Union has had of late, for no later than Monday they had a challenge from Mr. Brown, a respected member of St Bernard's, Edinburgh – their guarantee being only £3 or half-gate".

The letter additionally hinted that Crail had also arranged a challenge match against Third Lanark, at the time one of the top Scottish clubs!

Unfortunately, extensive research has failed to reveal if the challenge matches against Preston North End, who were at the time about to win the first-ever English League Championship (a title they retained the following season!) ever came off.

It is also unclear if Crail Union ever played St Bernard's, but what we do know for certain is that in April 1893 a side representing the famous Queen's Park (whose first team won the Scottish Cup that same year!) visited Crail for a challenge match against the Union and won by four goals without reply.

Crail Union participated only in challenge matches during their early days, but in January 1891 the club earned the distinction of hosting the first-ever cup-tie to be played in the East Neuk when Lochgelly visited the far-east of the county for a Cowdenbeath Cup second round fixture. Following a 1-1 draw, the Union were beaten 3-1 in the replay at Lochgelly.

Other cup competitions followed, including the East of Fife Badge, the Martin White Cup and the Kirkcaldy Cup. As for league football, the first such competition entered into by Crail was the East of Fife Football League, founded in 1892, which initially had six teams in its membership; the other clubs being Anstruther Rangers, Strathkinness Rangers, Cupar Athletic, Leven Thistle and St Andrews Athletic.

Crail Union eventually folded in 1907, but the name was eventually resurrected in 1919 with the formation of Crail Union Juniors; this second short-lived incarnation surviving until 1922.

Binnend Rangers

The once thriving village of Binnend, which clung to the slopes of the Binn Hill above Burntisland, was established during the early 1880's as a direct result of the influx of mine workers and their families who came to the area following the opening of the Binnend shale oil works in 1878.

Within a short period of time, the village boasted a school, a shop and a Free Church of Scotland mission hall, and from all accounts was a happy, thriving community, whose inhabitants enjoyed panoramic views across the Firth of Forth.

The Binnend Oil Works even boasted its own railway connection, which branched off from the main line at Kinghorn station!

The incomers hailed mainly from the West Lothian area, where the game of association football had been rapidly growing in popularity, and the miners wasted little time in establishing their own village football team, Binnend Rangers, who were founded around 1887 and initially played their home matches on Burntisland Links.

Football had already become well established in the Burntisland area by the time Binnend Rangers arrived on the scene and, despite being a junior club, the new village side weren't long in building up a fierce rivalry with local seniors Burntisland Thistle.

In one fiercely contested match between the sides, played at Thistle's home ground of LammerlawsPark in 1887, the Rangers took a first half lead amidst the loud cheers of their supporters.

The home side pressed hard for the equaliser, and with just nine minutes of the match remaining they finally managed to force the ball home. The referee, however, disallowed the goal for off-side, at which Thistle indignantly marched off the field in protest and refused to return, thus conceding the match to Binnend!

Eventually, the club was successful in securing a large enough piece of land to form a football field within the village itself, despite the fact that Binnend was situated high on the slopes of a hill and flat ground was at a premium!

This football field, however, appears to have fallen short of the standards deemed acceptable by visiting junior football clubs and, in 1889, following fund raising events which included a concert held at the "reading room" in Binnend, the club successfully secured the use of a better facility within the village.

In a letter to the 'Fifeshire Advertiser' in May 1889, a correspondent calling himself "One of the Eleven" was keen to spread the word about Binnend Rangers' new ground:

"SIR,- Any of the junior football clubs that has visited Binnend during this last season will be glad to hear that there is a new field in the course of preparation for next season, and we hope that it will be ready for the sports in July. That was the greatest obstacle that lay in the way of us having a better team".

The new and improved Binnend football ground would appear to have been a substantial enclosure, and was located at the foot of the village shale bing, which no-doubt doubled as a "grandstand" on match days!

As a junior club, Binnend Rangers competed regularly against other local junior teams including Rossland (Kinghorn), Kirkcaldy Fern, Kirkcaldy Albion, Lochgelly United and Inverkeithing Thistle.

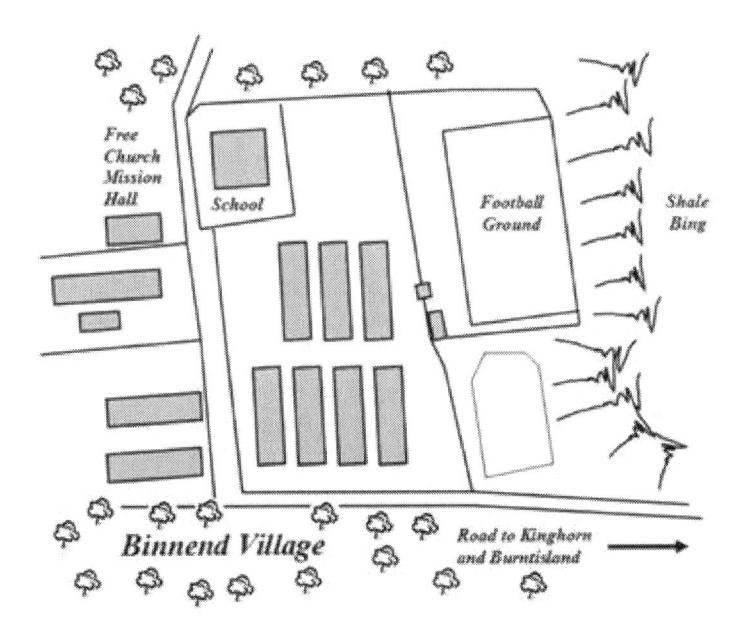

Binnend village, with the second football ground shown at the foot of the shale bing. It is possible that the original ground was located within the enclosure marked out just a few yards to the south.

The Rangers also competed in the Scottish Junior Cup, and in October 1892 lost narrowly in that competition by a single goal to Dunfermline Juniors; the same club that had made history when founded in 1874 as Fife's first-ever senior club before becoming the first Fife club to compete in the Scottish Cup (senior) in 1876.

Binnend Oil Works ceased operations in 1895 and the workforce were made redundant, but rather surprisingly Binnend village remained inhabited, and Binnend Rangers carried on, albeit as a juvenile club, until at least 1905.

Gradually, however, with Binnend lacking such basic services as running water, gas, electricity and sanitation, the population of the village began to decline as the twentieth century progressed.

Binnend village as seen from the shale bing. The south-west corner of the football ground can be seen at the bottom of the picture.

Binnend was formally declared closed in 1931, but some families refused to leave and held out for as long as they could. The village's last inhabitant remained until as late as 1954!

AncientCity Athletic

St. Andrews football side Ancient City Athletic, pictured in 1899.

Association football was late to arrive in St Andrews, with the game of rugby proving to be more popular as a spectator sport during the mid to late nineteenth century; the local university fifteen regularly playing attractive fixtures against other prominent Scottish rugby clubs including Edinburgh Academical, Edinburgh Wanderers and Aberdeen University to name but a few.

Traditionally, for those locals who had an inclination to participate in sport, the prevalence of golf in St Andrews made that sport the traditional choice of recreation, with association football rarely played in the town until the early 1880's.

Indeed, what may have been one of the first attempts to play association football in St Andrews took place in 1878, when it was reported that a "football match" had been staged on part of the golf course.

The match was reported to have taken place "eastward of the Swilcan Burn" in front of around 2,000 spectators, whereby, according to the 'Fife Herald', "golfing on the ground was rendered impossible".

Rugby was also commonly referred to as "football" in the newspapers of the mid to late 1800's, but as there was an abundance of rugby fields in the town at that time, there would surely have been no need to play rugby on the golf links, so there is the distinct possibility that this particular match was played under association rules.

During the 1880's, the first association football clubs were inaugurated in St Andrews, but the standard of football played by these clubs was not considered good enough for inter-club matches, and the members simply played games amongst themselves.

All this changed in March 1889, however, when it was decided to amalgamate the aforementioned clubs to form a team capable of competing with other clubs, and Ancient City Athletics Football Club was founded.

Unfortunately, the new club had no football ground on which to play home matches in its very early days. Although they had been granted the use of CliftonBankPark, which was the sports ground of a private school, the venue was unavailable on Saturday afternoons due to the school's own sports commitments, and AncientCity were only able to make use of the facility for training on weekday evenings.

AncientCity's first-ever match against another team, therefore, was played away from home against Whitecross from Guardbridge. Wearing their new colours of "black and white striped jerseys with blue knickers", the team's first outing was not a successful one, and resulted in a 7-1 defeat from their near neighbours.

On 14th September 1889, almost six months after the club's foundation, AncientCity played their first "home" match, against Dundee side Battlefield on StationPark, St Andrews, where the visitors emerged victorious by four-goals-to-two.

In season 1889/90, during which the club relocated to RathelpiePark, AncientCity played no fewer than twenty matches, of which six were won, twelve were lost, and two were drawn.

Some heavy defeats were sustained during the early part of that season, however, including a ten-nil hammering by Crail Union, but gradually the team improved and recorded more favourable results during the latter stages of the campaign to instill some confidence for the future.

However, when the following season was due to get under way, AncientCity once again found themselves without a home ground, and the club was forced into abeyance as far as inter-club fixtures were concerned.

The club's committee remained active despite the setback and, as well as organising several fund-raising events to maintain a healthy financial situation, successfully negotiated the use of a ground at Balgove, to the west of St Andrews, following an appeal in the local newspaper.

AncientCity moved into BalgovePark in February 1891 and a few matches were played at the venue as the club attempted to re-build the team over the following year, but it was not until season 1892/93, after the club moved back to RathelpiePark, that regular fixtures against other clubs were organised.

A flying start was made to the new season, with the team victorious in their first four matches; but the form was not to last, and only another three games were won before the end of the campaign, with nine of the eighteen matches played being lost and two drawn.

The standard of football now being played by AncientCity was gradually improving, however, and the club was comfortably engaging with teams of a higher standard on a regular basis.

The following season, 1893/94, Ancient City Athletic became members of the newly-founded East of Fife League, along with Leven Thistle, Vale of Leven, Cupar Athletic, Crail Union, Whitecross and Anstruther Rangers.

Although the league campaign got off to a poor start with a six-nil drubbing by Vale of Leven, the club rallied and, at end of the season, AncientCity had attained a mid-table position of fourth:

East of Fife Junior League Final Table (as near as can be ascertained), Season 1893/94:

	P	W	D	L	F	A	Pts
Cupar Athletic	11	7	2	2	37	16	12
Vale of Wemyss	8	5	2	1	29	13	12
Crail Union	9	5	1	3	34	27	11
AncientCity Athletic	9	4	1	4	17	26	9
Leven Thistle	9	3	1	5	18	27	7
Anstruther Rangers	7	1	1	5	7	17	3
White Cross	6	1	0	5	9	25	2

Alas, competing in the East of Fife League was considered to be too expensive for all the clubs involved, and at a meeting of the league committee on 17th September 1894 it was decided to abandon the competition.

The team's greatest achievement during season 1893/94, however, was the winning of the Martin White Cup at BonvilPark in Cupar, where a crowd of over 1,500 witnessed victory by the odd-goal-in-seven over old foes Crail Union on Saturday 24th March 1894.

Such was the interest in this match, special trains were run from both St Andrews and Crail to Cupar, with other "football enthusiasts" making their way to the county town by bicycle or horse and cart.

The final score was even sent by telegram to the 'St. Andrews Citizen' newspaper office, where it was posted in the window to the delight of the large crowd that had assembled there awaiting news of the event!

When the train carrying hundreds of supporters along with the team and cup arrived back in St. Andrews later that evening, captain Murray and the trophy were carried shoulder-high from the railway station to the Royal Hotel, where the team's success was toasted well into the night.

It was at this time that Ancient City were forced to re-locate once again, and this time secured the tenancy of Kinness Park, which was, as the name would suggest, in the vicinity of the Kinness Burn; the actual location of the ground being between the burn and the Lade Braes Walk at the western end of the town, roughly where Cockshaugh Park exists today.

Within a year, KinnessPark had been developed into the club's best ground to date, being fully enclosed within a wooden perimeter fence and boasting a grandstand.

With their new improved facilities, Ancient City were in a position to attract senior clubs to St Andrews for challenge matches, and within a short period of time Kinness Park had played host to the likes of St Johnstone and Dundee.

Other major crowd-pullers to visit St Andrews at this time included Scottish Junior Cup holders Parkhead as well as the highly-respected English club London Caledonian.

AncientCity Athletic were now going from strength to strength and, in October 1897, the club managed to raise a few eyebrows when they successfully persuaded Glasgow Celtic, league leaders at the time, to send their first team through to St. Andrews for a friendly which was billed as "The Greatest Football Match Ever Witnessed in the East of Fife".

The local press reacted with delight to the prospect and, on the Saturday preceding the match, the 'St. Andrews Citizen' commented:

"That such a treat was to be provided had never been dreamt of before this week, and until the match was advertised, people would scarcely credit the news."

On Monday 18th October, in front of a "disappointing" crowd of around one thousand (the Ancient City officials had decided to charge full Scottish League admission prices for the match!), the Scottish League side, as expected, ran out comfortable winners by four goals to one.

The event was, however, hailed as a great success, and was a clear indication that St Andrews was now well and truly on the football map less than a decade after organised association football had first come to the town!

AncientCity Athletic continued to grow from strength to strength, and won the Martin White Cup no fewer than five times during the first ten years of their existence as well as establishing themselves as a side to be reckoned with in the Scottish Junior Cup and the East of Scotland Cup.

GREATEST FOOTBALL MATCH

EVER WITNESSED IN THE EAST OF FIFE

WILL BE PLAYED AT

KINNESS PARK, ST.ANDREWS,

ON

MONDAY FIRST

(AUTUMN HOLIDAY)

CELTIC

(Full Scottish League Team)

v.

ANCIENT CITY ATHLETIC

KICK OFF 2:15 P.M.

Admission, 6d; Boys, 3d; Covered Stand, 3d extra

CELTIC TEAM –

McArthur
Welford,   Doyle.
Reynolds,   Goldie,   Orr.
Blessington, Campbell, Allan, McMahon, King

A reproduction of a poster produced for the event billed as the
"GREATEST FOOTBALL MATCH EVER WITNESSED IN THE EAST OF FIFE"

Unfortunately, the club was not as well supported by the local townsfolk as one would have expected despite St Andrews being one of the more heavily populated Fife towns at that time.

One of the reasons for this, it was repeatedly claimed by some locals, was that the Ancient City Athletic committee consistently looked for players from outside St Andrews, claiming that if the club wanted success on the park they would have to seek out the best players available from other towns and villages.

At the beginning of the 1899/1900 season, the committee finally succumbed to the theory that "home talent has sometimes needlessly been overlooked", and decided to recruit players solely from St Andrews in future, according to the 'St. Andrews Citizen' in an article printed on 22nd July 1899:

"The AncientCity Athletic Committee, we learn, have decided to choose their teams this season solely from players belonging to the city – a commendable step, in our opinion".

Unfortunately, this new signing policy had a detrimental effect on the team's performances on the park during the following season.

A home defeat at the hands of Buckhaven in the first round of the Dunfermline Cup was closely followed by a drubbing at the hands of Lochgelly in the Cowdenbeath Cup; and the club subsequently scratched from the two biggest cup competitions; the Scottish Cup and the East of Scotland Cup.

As for league football, some encouraging home form was displayed, including an 8-0 win over Tayport, but any encouragement this emphatic win may have given the team was blown away by a 9-2 reverse against Anstruther Rangers.

At the start of the following season, the committee announced that it was having difficulty raising a team, and it would appear that a certain amount of apathy had set in amongst the local footballers.

Eventually, however, a team was raised, and Ancient City Athletic took to the field once again, playing their first match of the season against Forthill Athletic on 13th September 1900.

Matches played during season 1900/01 were few and far between, however, and when a fierce gale in late December 1900 destroyed most of the fencing at KinnessPark and severely damaged the grandstand, it looked like the club was in danger of folding.

A meeting was called in January 1901 to decide on the best way forward, and it was decided that repairs to the fence and grandstand would be more than club's finances could stretch to. A month later, on Thursday 14th February, an article appeared in the 'Dundee Evening Post' which confirmed the club was about to be made homeless:

"The AncientCity barricading, grandstand & c., are to be sold by public auction on Saturday first. The club has given up KinnessPark, and does not intend putting up expensive fittings on another enclosure"

Despite having no home ground, AncientCity did manage to fulfill a few more fixtures before the end of the season, but the club was forced into abeyance for season 1901/02 due to a shortage of players in the town as well as a general sense of apathy.

The club was resurrected a year later under the name St Andrews City (although some match reports still referred to the club as Ancient City Athletic!), playing mainly friendly matches as and when they could be arranged.

Season 1903/04, despite starting badly with a nine-nil hammering from Vale of Wemyss in the East of Scotland Cup, eventually turned out to be a reasonably successful campaign, with City winning no fewer than four trophies.

The great days of Ancient City Athletic would never be seen again, however, and the club soldiered on under its new moniker without setting the heather alight until eventually folding during the First World War.

Leven F.C.

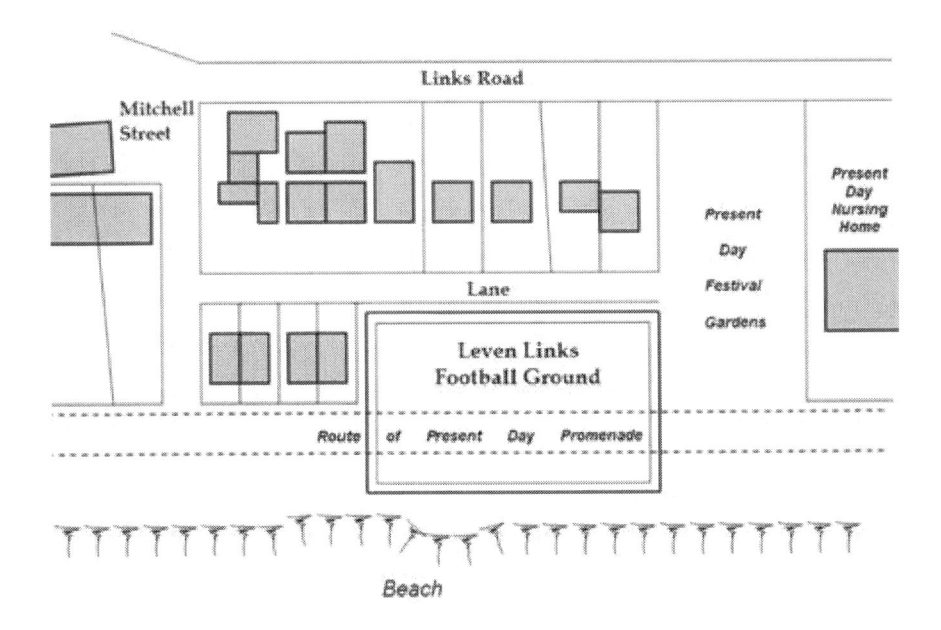

The location of Leven Links football ground, as far as can be determined using all available evidence.

During the summer of 1889, the footballers of Leven, who had until then played mainly within the ranks of local clubs Star of Leven and Vale of Leven, decided to form a senior club for the town, and duly applied for membership of the Fife Football Association.

The club's home ground was on Leven Links, and evidence suggests that it was located where there now exists an amusement arcade, immediately to the west of the FestivalGardens.

Amongst other clubs applying for membership of the association at this time were Raith Rovers, who had also decided to try their hand at the senior game after having played in the junior ranks since their inception six years earlier in 1883.

Leven's application was accepted (as was Raith's) and, for season 1889/90, the Fife Football Association boasted no fewer that thirteen members; namely Blairadam, Burntisland Thistle, Clackmannan, Cowdenbeath, Dunfermline, Fifeshire Hibernians (Lochgelly), Lassodie, Leven, Lochgelly Athletic, Raith Rovers, St Andrews University, Tillicoultry and Townhill (Dunfermline).

In preparation for their anticipated participation in that season's Fife Cup, Leven set up a series of challenge matches against local sides, but unfortunately the team and its followers soon built up an unenviable reputation, both on and off the field of play.

On Saturday 14th September 1889, Leven travelled up to the far-east of Fife to face Crail Union on Sauchope Links, but following the match the accusations started to fly that the referee (who incidentally hailed from Leven) had favoured the visiting team throughout the match, and had turned a blind eye to some decidedly heavy challenges from the Leven players.

It is also alleged that the referee, when one of the home side challenged him on a dubious decision, had replied that he would favour Crail when next he refereed a match involving the East Neuk side!

The Anstruther newspaper 'East of Fife Record', on Friday 20th September 1889, was quick to point the accusing finger at the Leven club, stating that:

"This was not football but rough play. The Union on different occasions were about to leave the field through the Leven lads using filthy language towards not only the players but the spectators. The Union are not likely to bring back this team to Crail in a hurry for the sake of their own good name as well as the game of football".

However, it would appear that although the Leven club had acquired an unfavourable reputation in certain quarters, there was a compassionate and benevolent side to their character, as on 28th September 1889 a benefit match was arranged against Kirkcaldy Wanderers in aid of the Mauricewood Pit disaster fund (the Mauricewood Pit was situated near Penicuik, south of Edinburgh; where, on 5th September 1889, an underground fire claimed the lives of 63 miners).

Although the Wanderers, probably Fife's top side at the time, were not at full strength for the match, this promised to be Leven's stiffest test so far as they prepared for their forthcoming Fife Cup tie with Burntisland Thistle; the draw for the first round of the tournament having been made at a meeting of the association on the previous Saturday.

A large crowd turned out for the match, which was played on Leven Links, and by all accounts the Leven side, who emerged victorious by two goals to one, gave a good account of themselves and were a team to be reckoned with, as is evident from the following extract taken from a report which appeared in the following edition of the 'Fifeshire Advertiser':

"Not withstanding the weight of their opponents, the Wanderers played a plucky game, and at half-time were only one goal down. In the second half they managed to equalise, but before the finish another point was put on against them, and they were beat by 2 to 1".

The report in the 'Fifeshire Advertiser' also gives a rare insight into the quality of the Leven players, and concludes, rather surprisingly, with a glowing testimony as to the welcoming nature of the Leven club, which is in complete contrast to what had appeared in previous press reports:

"The Leven custodian played well, as also did Staig at back. The halves were a good trio, Thornton (late of Bo'ness) being best. The forwards also showed good form. There was a large crowd present, and the result of a collection which was taken was that £3-1s was collected, which will be handed over to the Penicuik Disaster Fund.

The Wanderers speak highly of the treatment of the Leven club, and will be happy to go back again".

The amount raised for the disaster fund may have only been three pounds and five pence in today's money, but in 1889 this would have been a welcome boost for the cause!

Leven's Fife Cup tie with Burntisland Thistle, due to be played on Saturday 12th October, eventually went ahead on Leven Links a week later, after having been delayed through Thistle's requirement to play off an East of Scotland Shield tie against Dunfermline Athletic at East End Park.

Unfortunately, the reputation of the Leven club was once again called into question, as is quite clearly evident from the match report which appeared in the following edition of the 'Dunfermline Press':

"The game throughout was very disagreeable, the Leven players indulging in a good deal of rough play, the result of which was that Shoolbred of the Thistle received a severe injury to his knee. The Burntisland team, however, were quite able for the home club and won by 8 goals to 4".

It would appear that defeat in the first round of the only competition the club ever entered was too much for the players and officials to take, as there is no record of Leven F.C. taking part in any further matches.

Levenmouth's first attempt at establishing a senior football team for the area had lasted only a few months, but if the team had not given up so easily, could Leven Football Club have gone on to establish itself in the Scottish Football scene?

If that had been the case, would there ever have been the need to establish East Fife Football Club in the neighbouring town of Methil some fourteen years later as a senior side to represent the area? One can only speculate!

Lochgelly United

Lochgelly United pictured in season 1894/95 with the East of Scotland Consolation Cup.

Formed in May 1890 by the merger of Lochgelly Athletic and Fifeshire Hibernians, Lochgelly United competed only in friendly and cup matches during their early days. The cup competitions entered by the club were, however, of a high standard, and included the Scottish Cup, the King Cup, the East of Scotland Cup, the East of Scotland Consolation Cup and the Fife Cup.

Lochgelly United's first ground was School's Park, which was located where the Lochgelly Centre (a small theatre and concert venue) exists today. Initially, this ground was no more than a large undeveloped field, but the pitch was eventually surrounded by a perimeter fence to allow an admission fee to be charged.

The biggest and most important competition entered into during United's early years was the Scottish Cup, and in 1891 they were drawn to face Broxburn Shamrock in the first round, but subsequently scratched from the competition on the eve of the tie.

The following season, qualifying rounds were introduced for the Scottish Cup and, following a draw at Penicuik in the first qualifying round, United demolished the Lothian side 7-1 in the replay at School's Park to set up a clash with Stenhousemuir in round two. Unfortunately for United, the Fife team progressed no further in that season's tournament, with the 'Warriors' inflicting a heavy defeat by six goals to one.

It was to be season 1895/96 before Lochgelly United successfully negotiated the qualifying stages of the national competition, when a 2-1 home victory over Raith Rovers on 11th January 1896 looked to have secured a place in round two.

Raith protested, however, on the grounds that United's David Anderson was in fact a player by the name of David McLaren, who had turned out for Lochee United in the qualifying rounds! The complaint was upheld, and Raith convincingly won the replayed tie by five goals to two. After falling at the first hurdle at home to King's Park in season 1896/97, it was to be the early years of the twentieth century before the club again reached the first round proper of the Scottish Cup, when they were drawn at home to Falkirk on 11th January 1902.

United had by this time re-located to their new home ground of Reid's Park, located at the west end of the town on the south side of Lumphinnans Road, where a "large and enthusiastic crowd" turned out for the cup-tie, despite the nearby counter-attraction of Cowdenbeath's home Scottish Cup clash with Hearts. Unfortunately, despite putting up a good fight on the day, United went down by two goals without reply.

Lochgelly United eventually managed to reach the second round of the Scottish Cup for the first time by beating Inverness Caledonian 5-1 at home in January 1905, and were rewarded with a trip to Glasgow to face Celtic, where they went down by three-goals-to-nil in front of an extremely disappointing crowd of only 2,000!

Subsequent years in the Scottish Cup saw little success, and the furthest the club ever managed to progress in the competition was during season 1919/20, when they recorded first and second round victories over Inverness Clachnacuddin and Royal Albert before being drawn to face Third Lanark at home in round three on 21st February 1920. As expected the Glasgow side, who were at the time competing in the top half of the Scottish League, progressed to the quarter-final with victory by three goals to nil.

Lochgelly did cross swords with Celtic on one further occasion in the Scottish Cup, on 13th January 1923, by which time United were competing in the Second Division of the Scottish League. In front of a home crowd of over 10,000, the Fife team put up a brave fight, but eventually lost a closely-fought game by the odd-goal-in-five. Reporting on the match, the following day's edition of the 'Sunday Post' commented:

"Celtic had the fight of their lives with Lochgelly United in their tie, and with a little luck the Second Leaguers could have forced a replay".

Lochgelly also played the other half of the "Old Firm", Rangers, on two occasions in the national competition, losing 4-1 at Ibrox in 1924 and by 3-0 at the same venue in 1926.

As is evident from the earlier chapters in this book, the Fife Cup was considered to be a major trophy during the late nineteenth century and early twentieth century, but unfortunately for Lochgelly United they were "always the bridesmaids and never the brides" in this competition.

They did appear in the final eight times, however; the first occasion being in season 1893/94 when they lost heavily to Raith Rovers by six-goals-to-two at East End Park in Dunfermline following a hugely controversial series of matches against Kirkcaldy at the semi-final stage.

In the first of the aforementioned semi-final clashes, played at School's Park on Saturday 10th February 1894, both teams started the game having to contend with heavy underfoot conditions following several days of heavy rain. Despite the conditions, three goals were scored during the opening exchanges, and United were 2-1 ahead when the inclement weather started to get decidedly worse. With heavy rain falling and with the pitch starting to flood in places, the referee had no other option but to abandon the match with just twenty minutes played.

Two weeks later, the teams returned to the same venue to decide the tie, and what can only be described as an all-out brawl ensued!

The match throughout had been played in an extremely unsavoury manner, during which certain Lochgelly players were alleged to have:

"hacked and kicked the Kirkcaldy players in the most unmerciful and brutal manner."

It all came to ahead eight minutes from the end when, with Kirkcaldy four-goals-to-one ahead, the home crowd decided to join in the fight and rushed on to the field to remonstrate with some of the Kirkcaldy players, some of whom were: *"sent sprawling among the mud"* by the angry mob. *"Pandemonium reigned supreme"*, commented the following edition of the Kirkcaldy-based 'Fife Free Press'.

The same newspaper then went on to describe the ugly scenes in finite detail, and added that the referee, in an attempt to regain control, then:

"ordered some of the players to retire, and made a statement to the effect that the tie would not be proceeded with unless his orders were obeyed."

The Kirkcaldy side, however, refused to leave the field, demanding that the home side be disqualified. Of course, the matter of disqualification was not in the hands of the referee, and had to be referred to the Fifeshire Association. In support of their local side, the following edition of the 'Fife Free Press' carried the following comment:

"The matter will come for consideration at the Fife Association meeting on Saturday first, and it will indeed be a pity if that body does not make an example of the conduct indulged in by some of the Lochgelly players. It is high time that such scenes as were enacted on Saturday were put down by the "powers that be" with a firm hand, and, we have no doubt, the Association will see justice meted out."

The same newspaper, when summing up the ugly scenes, commented:

"The Kirkcaldy football team - as well as the supporters from the "Lang Toun" who accompanied them on Saturday to Lochgelly - will not be likely to forget in a hurry their semi-final tie in the Fife Cup with the Lochgelly United. Without exception, it was the most disgraceful football match, to our knowledge, witnessed in Fife for many a long day, and for the honour of the game it is be hoped a similar occurrence will never have to be recorded again".

However, before the matter came before the Fifeshire Association, Lochgelly United lodged a protest of their own, claiming that Kirkcaldy had fielded an ineligible player!

Rather surprisingly, the Fife Association ruled that Lochgelly would not be thrown out of the competition, and that the semi-final had to be replayed.

At the neutral venue of NorthEndPark in Cowdenbeath on Saturday 31st March, the cup-tie was eventually decided in favour of Lochgelly by three-goals-to-one in front of a "large crowd". Those spectators who had turned up hoping to see another brawl were to be disappointed, however, with the local press reporting following the match that:

"The game was never at any period of a particularly attractive nature, and those who witnessed it were certainly not much edified."

As previously stated, United were well-beaten by Raith Rovers in the final.

Lochgelly United's name could well have been inscribed on the trophy following their second Fife Cup final appearance in season 1898/99, when they played Raith Rovers at Stark's Park in front of 2,000 spectators on 6th May 1899.

The Lochgelly supporters came out in force for the match, and a special train was operated from Lochgelly to Kirkcaldy. The visiting supporters were also conveyed to the "scene of battle", according to the local press, by way of "brakes, waggonettes and cycles".

With conditions perfect for football, a hard-fought match ensued, which Raith eventually won by two-goals-to-nil. However, Lochgelly lodged a protest with the Fifeshire Association following the game, claiming that the referee had been "incompetent". A special meeting of the Association was called, and in Dunfermline on Wednesday 10th May it was unanimously decided that the match be replayed!

Raith Rovers, however, decided not to participate in the replayed match, which in effect handed the Fife Cup to Lochgelly United.

Despite this unexpected upturn in their fortunes, United refused to be declared winners of the competition in this manner and, instead of having their name inscribed on the trophy for what would have been their one and only time, opted to leave the Fife Cup tournament for season 1898/99 recorded as undecided!

The following season Lochgelly United had another chance to have their name inscribed on the trophy when both they and Dunfermline Athletic progressed to the Fife Cup Final. The tournament had been considerably weakened that season, however, with both Cowdenbeath and Raith Rovers deciding not to take part; the latter club's decision no doubt influenced by the decision of the Fife Association to nullify their Fife Cup win at the end of the previous season.

The final was played over two legs, with the first match at School's Park ending 2-2 and the second game at East EndPark finishing 3-3. A third meeting between the two clubs to decide the cup winners was therefore required, but for some reason was never played, so for the second successive year the destination of the Fife Cup was left unresolved.

In the early years of the twentieth century, Lochgelly United reached the Fife Cup final on a further three occasions, only to lose to East Fife in 1908 and Cowdenbeath in both 1910 and 1926.

As for other cup competitions, the first silverware annexed by Lochgelly United was the East of Scotland Consolation Cup, which was won in season 1894/95, when Cowdenbeath were overcome in the final at neutral East EndPark in Dunfermline. In lesser cup competitions, United were Wemyss Cup winners four times, in 1902, 1903, 1922 and 1924.

In league football, Lochgelly were admitted to the newly-formed six-team Central League at the beginning of the 1896/97 season along with Kirkcaldy, Cowdenbeath, Dunfermline Athletic, St. Johnstone and Fair City Athletic (Perth).

Their participation in the Central League during the first season of that particular competition, however, was rather apathetic to say the least, with arranged fixtures being few and far between.

It would appear that Lochgelly United preferred to compete in cup competitions, as did most clubs at that time, with league fixtures reserved for blank Saturdays when participation in all knock-out tournaments had been exhausted. This resulted in the Central League's first season ending in an almost complete wash-out!

Consequently, the Central League was not started at the beginning of season 1897/98, but following a meeting held in Dunfermline in November 1897, the decision was made to re-introduce the competition, which eventually got under way with seven participating clubs, namely Alloa Athletic, Cowdenbeath, Dundee Reserves, Dunfermline Athletic, Hearts of Beath, Kirkcaldy and Lochgelly United. United did make more of an effort to fulfil their fixtures in the re-vamped competition, but only managed to win two league matches before the end of the season.

Deciding that league football wasn't really for them, Lochgelly United resorted to participating in knock-out cup tournaments and challenge matches for the remainder on the nineteenth century. It was to be the 1902/03 season before the club decided to enter league competition once again, and were duly admitted to the Northern League, in which they finished runners-up to Dundee Reserves at the first time of asking.

It was at this time that Lochgelly decided to develop their Reid's Park ground, which they had secured tenancy of in 1901, by adding a 400-seat grandstand, the first such facility to be enjoyed by the club's supporters.

Just five years later, however, the club was forced to move once again when building work encroached on Reid's Park, and United found themselves back in the centre of town at

Recreation Park, which was situated adjacent to their original School's Park home.

This was undoubtedly Lochgelly's best ground to date, being fully enclosed with a grandstand constructed on the north side of the pitch and having a stated capacity of 15,000.

United's membership of the Northern League continued until season 1909/10, when they became members of the re-formed Central League along with Alloa Athletic, Arbroath, Bathgate, Bo'ness, Broxburn Athletic, Dunfermline Athletic, East Fife, King's Park, Kirkcaldy United and St. Johnstone.

A financial crisis attributed to a miners' strike during the 1911/12 season almost forced United out of business, and the club was forced to leave the Central League when they could not fulfill their fixtures. They survived, however, and duly re-entered the Northern League for the following season. Against all the odds, Lochgelly's financial situation improved and they were re-admitted to the Central League for season 1913/14.

Incredibly, just over two years after almost going to the wall, Lochgelly United were admitted to the Scottish League at the beginning of the following season. Their Scottish League status was short-lived, however, as the outbreak of the Great War in 1914 forced the abandonment of the Scottish Second Division at the end of the 1914/15 campaign.

After competing in the wartime Eastern League for the duration of the war, United were re-admitted to the Central League once the hostilities had ceased. Two seasons later, the Central League in effect became the Second Division of the Scottish League, and consequently United were national league members for a second time. The club struggled to make their mark in the competition, however, and were relegated to the recently-formed Third Division at the end of the 1923/24 season.

When that league was abandoned just two years later, the writing was on the wall for Lochgelly United, and after only two seasons competing in the Scottish Alliance and minor cup competitions, the club was wound up in 1928.

United's Recreation Park ground was eventually built over by the houses in Timmon's Park and Dewar Street, with nothing now remaining to indicate that a Scottish League venue once existed on the site.

Other Notable Nineteenth Century Fife Football Clubs

There were several other football clubs founded in the late nineteenth century that have proved more difficult to research than the clubs whose histories are contained within the pages of this publication.

It could well be that some of these clubs also have interesting stories to tell, and perhaps further research will reveal tales similar to those related in this book!

The obvious exceptions are Fife's current Scottish League sides Cowdenbeath, Dunfermline Athletic and Raith Rovers, whose individual histories have been published in various forms since these clubs were founded in the late nineteenth century. The Kingdom's other current Scottish League side, East Fife, were not founded until the early twentieth century.

The senior clubs that existed in Fife in the late nineteenth century, other than those described in this book, are listed on the following pages in alphabetical order. However, the writer does not claim that the list is comprehensive!

Blairadam were one of the ten founder members of the Fifeshire Football Association. The club was based at SeefarPark in Kelty, and were members of the Fifeshire Football Association for three years until reverting to junior status in 1885. The club re-joined the Fife Association in 1887, but lasted only two seasons before joining the junior ranks once again. Records suggest that Blairadam had another brief flirt with the senior game again in the 1890's, but the club had disappeared from the football map completely by the end of the nineteenth century.

Broomhall were founded in 1882 in the west Fifevillage of Charlestown. They joined the Fifeshire Association in 1884 and competed in the Fife Cup for two seasons before reverting to junior status in 1886. They remained a junior club until being disbanded in 1925, and were members of the Fife Junior League from 1919 to 1925. Broomhall played their home matches on a public park in the centre of the village.

Cowdenbeath F.C. are to this day one of the better-known Fife football teams, and still play their home matches in the west-Fife former mining town. Formed in 1882 from the merger of Fife Football Association founder members Cowdenbeath Rangers and Raith Rovers (a Cowdenbeath team who had nothing to do with the Kirkcaldy team of the same name!); the club were admitted to the Fife Association in the year of their formation. Apart from brief spells during the two world wars, Cowdenbeath have been Scottish League members since 1905. The club has had a long and eventful history which is too detailed to relate in this one paragraph!

Cowdenbeath Our Boys were founded in 1885 and were immediately admitted to the Fifeshire Association. They lasted only one season, however, before disappearing without trace.

Dunfermline Athletic, like Cowdenbeath, are a well-known club in Scottish football circles to the present day. Founded in 1885 by a group of rebellious Dunfermline F.C. players, the details of which are contained in an earlier chapter within this book, the Athletic were admitted to the Fife Association in the year of their formation. Originally admitted to the Scottish League in 1912, they were forced to drop out due to the Great War three years later. The club was re-admitted in 1921 and, save for the interlude brought about by the Second World War, have been members ever-since.

The 'Pars' are one of only two Fife clubs to have won the Scottish Cup (the other club being East Fife, founded in 1903), and won the trophy in 1961 and again in 1968. They are also one of only two Fife clubs to have competed in Europe (the other being Raith Rovers), with the club reaching the European Cup Winners' Cup semi-final in season 1968/69.

Like the other senior Fife clubs still in existence, however, their rich history cannot be related in the small space available on this page!

Dunfermline Our Boys were members of the Fifeshire Football Association for just one season, 1883/84. They reverted to junior status, and played as such until 1888. The name was resurrected in 1900, and a team of that moniker had a brief association with the East of Scotland Junior League until 1902.

Dunfermline United had been, according to some records, founded in 1875, just a year after Dunfermline F.C. Like their fellow townsmen, United were founder members of the Fife Association, but only remained so until the end of the 1882/83 season. It could well be that a 12-2 defeat from their local rivals in that season's Fife Cup competition proved to be too much for the United players and officials to take!

Cowdenbeath Rangers were also one of the ten founder members of the Fifeshire Football Association, but before the first Fife Cup tournament got under way the club merged with the other Cowdenbeath senior club, Raith Rovers, to form the present-day Cowdenbeath Football Club.

Fifeshire Hibernians hailed from Lochgelly, and were founded in 1889 by a group of Irishmen who were at the time resident in Cowdenbeath. The club successfully applied to join the Fifeshire Association that same year. They played their home matches on a pitch close to the 'Fair Helen' coal pit, at the west end of the town. They lasted only one season, however, before merging with Lochgelly Athletic to form Lochgelly United in May 1990.

Halbeath is a village located a couple of miles to the east of Dunfermline. Their football team joined the Fifeshire Association in the year of their formation, 1883, and competed in the Fife Cup for two seasons without setting the heather alight, before being disbanded in 1885. Over ninety years later, the name re-appeared in Fife football circles when a junior team from the village were members of the Fife Junior League from 1976 until 1992.

Hearts of Beath stepped up to the senior ranks in 1897, some fourteen years after their foundation as a junior club, and joined the Fifeshire Association that same year. The club were based in Hill of Beath, immediately to the west of Cowdenbeath, and played in various senior competitions during the early years of the twentieth century. They retained their senior status until 1913, and during that time won the Fife Cup on two occasions; in season 1900/01 and again in 1902/03. After reverting to junior status, they played on until disappearing from the Fife football map completely during the early years of World War Two.

Kingseat, a village situated around two miles to the north of Dunfermline, boasted a senior football club founded in 1883. They were members of the Fife Football Association for the first six years of their existence, but resigned from the association in 1889 following a dispute. In 1894, Kingseat merged with near-neighbours Lassodie to form the short-lived Loch Rangers.

Kirkcaldy Rangers were first mentioned in the sports columns of the local press in October 1884, when they earned the distinction of being the first-ever club to play fellow Kirkcaldy club Raith Rovers, who they defeated by five-goals-to-nil on an open field where the local golf course now exists. They were admitted to the Fifeshire Association in 1885, but were members for just one season. They reverted to junior status for a few seasons, and a club of that name played in various forms until the early years of the twentieth century.

Loch Rangers were founded in 1894 from the merger of near-neighbours Kingseat and Lassodie. They were members of the East of Scotland Football Association for just one season, 1894/95.

Lochgelly Athletic were founded in 1886 and played their home matches at CooperhallPark before moving to School's Park in 1889. They joined the Fifeshire Football Association in 1888 and two years later merged with local rivals and fellow Fife association members Fifeshire Hibernians to form Lochgelly United.

Lumphinnans, a mining village situated between Cowdenbeath and Lochgelly, had a senior club founded in 1885. They joined the Fifeshire Association in the year of their formation, and were members for three seasons until 1888. The village boasted a junior club of the same name in season 1890/91 and again just after the turn of the century. Records show that a senior club under the Lumphinnans moniker was reincarnated for a brief period just before the Great War, but only played a handful of games.

Raith Rovers, like the aforementioned current Scottish League sides Cowdenbeath and Dunfermline Athletic, have a long history that simply cannot be diluted into a few lines on this page. As mentioned earlier in this book, Rovers were founded in 1884 and stepped up to the senior ranks in 1889. Raith were the first Fife club to gain admission to the Scottish League in 1902, and have been members ever since, save for a brief period during the Great War and also for the duration of the Second World War. The biggest trophy win in their history was the winning of the Scottish League Cup in 1995; an achievement which qualified the club for European competition in the form of the following season's UEFA Cup.

Raith Rovers (Cowdenbeath) were in existence before their Kirkcaldy namesakes, having been founded in 1881. Very little is known about this club, apart from the fact that they were founder members of the Fifeshire Football Association and merged with Cowdenbeath Rangers in June 1882 to form the present-day Cowdenbeath Football Club.

Rossend F.C. were founded in Burntisland in 1880 and became founder members of the Fife Football Association in 1882. They have the distinction of participating in the first-ever Fife Cup tie in September 1882, when they went down 4-1 to Cowdenbeath. Their merger with Burntisland Thistle in 1885 is detailed within the pages of this book.

St. Andrews University were admitted to the Fife Association in 1889. The club was officially founded in 1887, although at least one source hints that they could have been formed two years earlier. The 'Varsity have had a sporadic association with the Fife Association over the years, and were regular participants in both the Fife Cup and the Wemyss Cup in the years between the two World Wars. Their main claim to fame was the winning the Queen's Park Shield, a trophy competed for by the Scottish Universities, on three occasions, in 1925, 1926 and 1943.

St. Leonard's were formed around March 1882 in Dunfermline, and were founder members of the Fifeshire Football Association. Their home ground was stated as 'Towngreen', near the present-day East End Park, which was presumably surrounded by a fence of sorts, as the club was able to charge an admission fee of 3d (1 ½ pence in today's money). St. Leonard's dropped out of the Fife Association before the start of the 1885/86 season, however; their demise possibly triggered by the aftermath of their 22-0 defeat at the hands of Dunfermline F.C. in a Fife Cup tie on 11th October 1884.

Townhill, a village situated on high ground to the north of Dunfermline, boasted a senior football team from 1886 until the club reverted to junior status in or around 1890. They were members of the Fife Association for four seasons, but failed to make their mark in the Fife Cup during this time. They stepped up to the senior ranks again in 1894 after recruiting several players from Dunfermline Athletic, who had gone into temporary abeyance. They reached the semi-final of the 1894/95 Fife Cup, but failed to re-appear in any form the following season. The village had the occasional flirt with junior football, but Townhill's last junior club folded in 1925.

Vale of Forth hailed from North Queensferry, and were one of the ten founder members of the Fifeshire Football Association. They were founded at least as early as 1880, as they played a home match against Dunfermline United in December of that year. Vale dropped out of the Fife Association before the very first Fife Cup was competed for in season 1882/83, despite having become members just a couple of months earlier.

Former Fife Football Association Members from Fife's Neighbouring Counties

During the late nineteenth century, the Fifeshire Association admitted a number of clubs from Fife's neighbouring counties to its membership.

They were:

Clackmannanshire:

Alloa Athletic (Fife Cup winners in 1886); Alloa United; Clackmannan (Fife Cup winners in 1895 and 1896); Sauchie Volunteers; Tillicoultry; Vale of Forth (from Alloa, not to be confused with the North Queensferry club of the same name); and Wellington (Alloa).

Kinross-shire:

Loch Leven Rangers (Kinross); and Orwell (Milnathort).

Perthshire:

Fair City Athletic (Perth); and St. Johnstone (The same club that currently competes in the Scottish Football League. They were the last non-Fife side to compete in the Fife Cup in season 1899/1900).

Sources and Bibliography

The greatest source of information regarding Fife football clubs in the nineteenth and early twentieth centuries was gained by spending many hours perusing the newspapers that are held on microfilm in the various Fife libraries, including those at Anstruther, Cupar, Methil, Kirkcaldy, Cowdenbeath and Dunfermline.

The vast range of newspapers available on the British Newspaper Archive internet web site also proved to be a valuable source of information.

In addition, a number of books were occasionally referred to during many enjoyable hours of research.

These publications were:

Raith Rovers F.C.: A Centenary History (John Litster, 1983)

The Breedon Book of Scottish Football Records (Gordon Smailes, Breedon Books, 1995)

Rejected F.C. of Scotland, Volume 3 (Dave Twydell, Yore Publications,)

That's Fife: The History of the Fifeshire Football Association and the Fife Cup (David A. Allan, Cowdenbeath, 2015)

If you enjoyed this book, you might also enjoy the following publications by James K. Corstorphine, both of which are available in both paperback and eBook format from Amazon.co.uk:

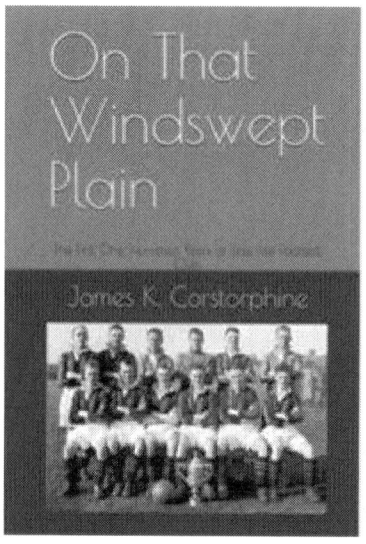

On That Windswept Plain

The First 100 Years

of

East Fife
Football Club

ISBN: 9781976888618

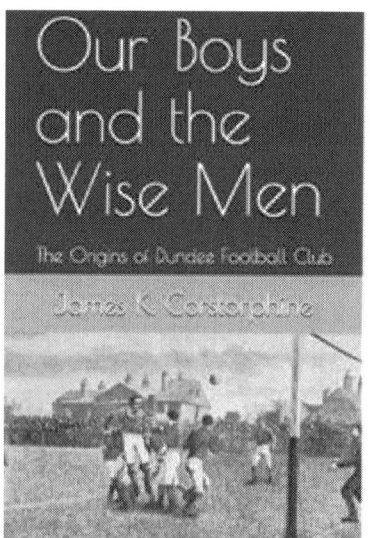

Our Boys
and the
Wise Men:

The origins of
Dundee Football Club

ISBN: 9798643521549

Other Publications available from Wast-By Books:

East of Thornton Junction: The Story of the FifeCoast Line

(James K. Corstorphine, 1995)

ISBN: 9781976909283

Dyker Lad: Recollections of Life in an East Neuk of FifeFishingVillage

(Alexander 'Sonny' Corstorphine, 2018)

ISBN 9781981019137

**The Saturday Sixpence and other tales:
A collection of short stories set in a fictional Scottish seaside town during the 1960's**

(James Kingscott, 2020)

ISBN 9798556376090

A Selection of Poems by 'Poetry Peter' Smith, the Fisherman Poet of Cellardyke

(Compiled by James K. Corstorphine, 2000)

ISBN 9798644727827

All of the above titles are available in both Paperback and Kindle eBook formats from: **amazon.co.uk**

Just one more thing before you go . . .

Your opinion would be very much appreciated!

I would be most grateful if you could find a few minutes to rate this book on Amazon.

I will take the time to read any comments made, and any suggestions as to how I can improve the publication will be taken on board.

Thank you!

James Corstorphine

Printed in Great Britain
by Amazon